# Inspirational Quotes

## 1000 Beautiful Quotes on Happiness, Love and Success

### Jason James

PUBLISHED BY:
Jason James
Copyright © 2013

**spisharam/flickr**
http://www.flickr.com/photos/11510574@N02/2971277927/in/photolist

1. "Use what talents you possess; the woods would be very silent if no birds sang there except those that sang best." -Henry Van Dyke

2. "Always be a first-rate version of yourself, instead of a second-rate version of somebody else." -Judy Garland

3. "No one can make you feel inferior without your consent." -Eleanor Roosevelt

4. "The world has the habit of making room for the man whose words and actions show that he knows where he is going." -Napoleon Hill

5. "It is the mark of an educated mind to be able to entertain a thought without accepting it." -Aristotle

6. "There appears to be a positive correlation between an atmosphere of 'human playfulness' (otherwise known as humor) in the workplace and the improvement of 'innovative activity and creativity'." -Observer Business

7. "Here on the edge of the twenty-first century, a fundamental new rule of business is that the Internet changes everything." -Bill Gates

8. "In the life of a man, his time is but a moment, his being an incessant flux, his senses a dim rushlight, his body a prey of worms, his soul an unquiet eddy, his fortune dark, and his fame doubtful. In short, all that is of the body is as coursing waters, all that is of the soul as dreams and vapors: life a warfare, a brief sojourning in an alien land; and after repute, oblivion. Where, then, can man find the power to guide and guard his steps? In one thing and one alone: philosophy."-Marcus Aurelius

9. "In the global marketplace of tomorrow, the successful company will be known for the quality of the employee that it keeps rather than the numbers of workers who are laid-off." -Morton Bahr

10. "The first rule in opera is the first rule in life: see to everything yourself." -Dame Nellie Melba

11. "I wouldn't like to have lived without ever having disturbed anyone." -Charles Urnick

12. "Intelligence is of the essence in warfare - it is what the armies depend upon in their every move...To be reliable, information

must be firsthand …There is thus an important relationship between intelligence and timing." -Sun-tzu

13.  "Don't waste your time on jealousy. Sometimes you're ahead, sometimes you're behind. The race is long and, in the end, it's only with yourself." -Mary Schmich

14.  "Astronomers estimate that there are at least 100 billion stars in the Milky Way" ('our' galaxy) and "It is estimated that 100 billion galaxies are in principle visible to our modern instruments." -John Gribbin

15.  "A memorandum is written not to inform the reader but to protect the writer." -Dean Acheson

16.  "At the heart of science is an essential balance between two seemingly contradictory attitudes - an openness to new ideas, no matter how bizarre or counterintuitive, and the most ruthlessly sceptical scrutiny of all ideas, old and new." -Carl Sagan

17.  "A life is never ended until all the lives it has touched have ended too." -Chinese proverb

18.  "When a man has once broken through the paper walls of everyday circumstance, those unsubstantial walls that hold so many of us securely prisoned from the cradle to the grave, he has made a discovery. If the world does not please you, you can change it. Determine to alter it at any price, and you can change it altogether. You may change it into something sinister and angry, to something appalling, but it may be you will change it to something brighter, more agreeable, and at the worst something much more interesting." -H.G. Wells

Moyan Brenn/flickr
http://www.flickr.com/photos/28145073@N08/6930842224/in/photolist

19. "The wealth of the three richest people in the world exceeds the combined GDP of the 48 smallest countries."-Guardian

20. "Five frogs are sitting on a log. Four decide to jump off. How many are left? There are still five - because there's a difference between deciding and doing."-Mark L Feldman

21. "There are only two ways to handle tense situations: you can change them, or you can change the way you look at them. There is enlightenment to be had in changing the way you look at things."-Paul Wilson

22. "Every breath you take contains atoms forged in the blistering furnaces deep inside stars. Every flower you pick contains atoms blasted into space by stellar explosions that blazed brighter than a billion suns. Every book you read contains atoms blown across unimaginable gulfs of space and time by the wind between the stars."-Marcus Chown

23. "It's no longer about the big beating the small; it's about the fast beating the slow." -Larry Carter

24. "Make a point of connecting with someone new every day. And re-acquaint yourself with anyone you have not spoken to for some time by going through your address book."-Roy Sheppard

25. "Life is like that old Spanish saying: 'He who plants the lettuce doesn't always eat the salad'." -Sunday Express

26. "Enthusiastic people are the ones who actually get things done in this world. Enthusiasm is what turns any idea into reality. And enthusiasm is linked closely with happiness."-Roy Sheppard

27. "Where, after all, do universal human rights begin? In small places close to home - so close and so small that they cannot be seen on any map of the world. Yet they are the world of the individual person: the neighborhood he lives in; the school or college he attends; the factory, farm or office where he works. Such are the places where every man, woman and child seeks equal justice, equal opportunity, equal dignity without discrimination. Unless these rights have meaning there, they have little meaning anywhere."-Eleanor Roosevelt

28. "There is always a little more toothpaste in the tube. Think about it." -Bill Bryson

29. "We shrink from change; yet is there anything that can come into being without it? What does nature hold dearer or more proper to herself? Could you have a hot bath unless the firewood underwent some change? Could you be nourished if the food suffered no change? Is it possible for any useful thing to be achieved without change?" -Marcus Aurelius

30. "You see things that are and say 'Why?' But I dream of things that never were and say 'Why not?"-George Bernard Shaw

31. "We... live in a world that has seen Superman, in the person of Christopher Reeve, rendered a quadriplegic, and a quadriplegic, in the person of Stephen Hawking, rendered Superman." - David Beresford

32. "There is no activity more intrinsically globalizing than trade, no ideology less interested in nations than capitalism, no challenge to frontiers more audacious than the market." - Benjamin R. Barber

33. "Two men look out through the same bars;
One sees the mud and one sees the stars." -Frederick Langbridge

34. "Indulge yourself by being generous - help someone out, perform an act of kindness, offer a compliment. The person who will feel most uplifted by you having done so is ...you." - Paul Wilson

35. "The doers cut a path through the jungle, the managers are behind them sharpening the machetes. The leaders find time to think, climb the nearest tree, and shout 'Wrong jungle!' Find time to climb the trees." -Peter Maxwel

36. "You've got to search for the hero inside yourself. Search for the secrets you hide. Search for the hero inside yourself - until you find the key to your life."-M People

37. "Words open the soul's window to ideas and the discourse of words is how we grope our way to conversation and, when conversation can be stripped of its inequalities and hidden

hegemonies, how we eventually become capable of cooperation, of common life with others, and even of justice." -Benjamin R.

38. "The only one who got everything done by Friday was Robinson Crusoe."-Mirror

39. "Ask most people which is the dominant language on planet Earth and they will reply that it's either English or Chinese. A good guess, but they would be wrong. Binary is now dominant, with computers and machines having more conversations every working day than a sum total of mankind going back to the birth of Eve." -Peter Cochrane

40. "In spite of illness, in spite of the arch enemy sorrow, one can remain alive long past the usual date of disintegration if one is unafraid of change, insatiable of intellectual curiosity, interested in big things, and happy in small ways."-Edith Wharton

41. "Creative work will increasingly involve people working in teams which combine members with different skills and backgrounds. These teams are more effective when people can trust fellow team members to play their part. In low-trust organizations, people will tend to hoard knowledge and only share ideas formally through memos and when requested. In high-trust organizations, people are more likely to bestow their knowledge on one another and develop joint understandings of problems and their solutions. Trust and co-operation will be vital to the work cultures of the future." -Charles Leadbeater

42. "We are all molded and remolded by those who have loved us and, though that love may pass, we remain, none the less, their work. No love, no friendship can ever cross the path of our destiny without leaving some mark upon it forever."-Francois Mauriac

43. "To be cheerful about 2000, consider only this. Of the 30 major elections that will be held, 16 will be in countries that 25 years ago were dictatorships." -Economist

44. "Our feelings of dissatisfaction, unhappiness, loss of hope and so forth are in fact related to all phenomena. If we do not adopt the right outlook, it is possible that anything and everything could cause us frustration. Yet phenomena are part of reality and we are subject to the laws of existence. So this leaves us only one option: to change our own attitude. By bringing about a change in our outlook towards things and events, all phenomena can become friends or sources of happiness, instead of becoming enemies or sources of frustration." -Dalai Lama

45. "Problems cannot be solved by thinking within the framework in which they were created." -Albert Einstein

46. "Two roads diverged in a wood, and I -
I took the one less travelled by.
And that has made all the difference." -Robert Frost

47. "Never doubt that a small group of thoughtful, committed people can change the world. Indeed it is the only thing that ever has." -Margaret Mead

48. "There is an emerging consensus about what the knowledge-creating company of the future will look like. It will be good at learning and unlearning. It will be open to new ideas from a diverse network of contacts, but able to integrate them smoothly, with the financial, production and marketing skills needed to make money from them. Staff will have a large measure of autonomy to try and fail. Employees will be encouraged to challenge the status quo. Open communication and information-sharing with customers, staff and suppliers will

encourage a flow of ideas. Teamwork and flexibility will be taken for granted." -Charles Leadbeater

49. "Never assume, as assume makes an ass out of u and me." - Mirror

50. "By 2020, we will have synthetic intelligent life forms sharing our planet and they may even have legal rights. They will catch up with human intelligence before then in overall terms, though there will still be a few things left that only humans can do. Most new knowledge will be developed by synthetic intelligence and we will have to accept that we just do not understand some of it, while accepting the resultant benefits." - Ian Pearson

51. "This time, like all times, is a very good one if we but know what to do with it." -Ralph Waldo Emerson

52. "There is therefore no function in society which is peculiar to woman as woman or man as man; natural abilities are similarly distributed in each sex and it is natural for woman to share all occupations with men." -Plato

53. "Academics have now confirmed what many of us have long believed: that positive thinking leads to a longer and healthier life." -Observer Magazine

54. "The Web must allow equal access to those in different economic and political situations; those who have physical or cognitive disabilities; those of different cultures; and those who use different languages with different characters that read in different directions across a page." -Berners-Lee

**55.** "Everything should be made as simple as possible, but not simpler."-Albert Einstein

**56.** "When you would have a cordial for your spirits, think of the good qualities of your friends."-Marcus Aurelius

**57.** "My country is the world and my religion is to do good." -Thomas Paine

**58.** "Most smiles are started by another smile." -Anonymous

**59.** "Truth will prevail." -Jan Hus

**60.** "Some men die in shrapnel
Some go down in flames
Most men perish inch by inch
Playing little games." -John O'Keeffe

61. "The one important thing that I have learned over the years is the difference between taking one's work seriously and taking one's self seriously. The first is imperative and the second is disastrous." -Margot Fonteyn

62. "The mind is not a vessel to be filled, but a fire to be ignited." -Delphic Oracle

63. "You're either part of the solution or part of the problem." -Eldridge Cleaver

64. "We tend to measure life by too one-sided a standard: its length rather than its greatness; we think more of extending life than of filling it." -Tomas Masaryk

65. "There is good evidence that how long you sleep seems to be the most important indicator of how long you'll live."-William C. Dement

66. "Most people don't take the time to think. I made an international reputation for myself by deciding to think twice a week." -George Bernard Shaw

67. "The purpose of life is a life of purpose." -John O'Keeffe

68. "We act as though comfort and luxury were the chief requirements of life, when all we need to make us really happy is something to be enthusiastic about." -Charles Kingsley

69. "Neither fire nor wind, birth nor death can erase our good deeds." -Buddha

70. "There is no such thing on earth as an uninteresting subject; the only thing that can exist is an uninterested person." -G.K. Chesterton

71. "Life is made up of giving and getting and forgiving and forgetting." -Anonymous

72. "When I give food to the poor, they call me a saint. When I ask why the poor have no food, they call me a communist." -Dom HelderCamara

73. "To live each day as though one's last, never flustered, never apathetic, never attitudinizing - here is the perfection of character." -Marcus Aurelius

74. "Nothing will ever be attempted if all possible objections must first be overcome." -Dr Samuel Johnson

75. "The 21st century corporation must adapt itself to management via the Web. It must be predicated on constant change, not stability; organized around networks, not rigid hierarchies; built on shifting partnerships and alliances, not self-sufficiency; and constructed on technological advantages, not bricks and mortar." - John A Byrne

76. "Many people would die sooner than think; in fact, they do."- Bertrand Russell

77. "If we work upon marble it will perish; if on brass, time will efface it; if we rear temples, they will crumble into dust; but if we work upon immortal minds, and imbue them with principles, with the just fear of God and love of our fellow man, we will engrave on those tablets something that will brighten all eternity." -Noah Webster

78. "He has not learned the lesson of life who does not every day surmount a fear."-Ralph Waldo Emerson

79. "We are made of stardust. Every atom of every element in your body except for hydrogen has been manufactured inside stars, scattered across the universe in great stellar explosions and recycled to become part of you." -John Gribbin

80. "The humane do not worry; the wise are not perplexed; and the courageous do not feel fear." —Confucius

81. "More than 300 million people in the world speak English and the rest, it sometimes seems, try to." -Bill Bryson

82. "One who loses money, loses much; one who loses a friend, loses much more; one who loses faith, loses all." -Anonymous

83. "Injustice anywhere is a threat to justice everywhere." -Martin Luther King

84. "Three passions, simple but overwhelmingly strong, have governed my life: the longing for love, the search for knowledge, and unbearable pity for the suffering of mankind." -Bertrand Russell

85. "It is only with the heart that one sees rightly; what is essential is invisible to the eye." -Antoine de Saint-Exupéry

86. "One does not worry about the fact that other people do not appreciate one. One worries about not appreciating other people." —Confucius

87. "Women have become terribly important to me. Not that I understand them. I just like the tangible comfort they give me and their different point of view." -Peter O'Toole

88. "I believe that a lot of our striving after the symbols and levers of success is due to a basic insecurity, a need to prove ourselves.

That done, grown up at last, we are free to stop pretending." -
Charles Handy

89. "The trouble with the rat-race is that, even if you win, you're still a rat."-Lily Tomlin

90. "Do, or do not. There is no 'try'." -Strikes Back

91. "Even a little gift may be vast with loving kindness." - Theocritus

92. "If you want to be happy for a short time, get drunk; happy for a long time, fall in love; happy for ever, take up gardening." - Arthur Smith

93. "True fulfilment is, I believe, vicarious. We get our deepest satisfaction from the fulfilment, growth and happiness of others. It takes time, often a lifetime, to realize this." -Charles Handy

94. "We have to free half of the human race, the women, so that they can help to free the other half." -Emmeline Pankhurst

95. "Ask a question and you're a fool for three minutes; do not ask a question and you're a fool for the rest of your life." - Anonymous

96. "I don't think you can change the world by smashing up McDonald's - but I do believe that you can change the world by organizing a trade union in McDonald's." -Billy Bragg

97. "Today we know that the greatest danger is not the evil among those who are evil, but the silence of those who are good." - GöranPersson

**98.** "The only thing that does not change is that everything changes." -Adeline Yen Mah

**99.** "Great minds discuss ideas; average minds discuss events; small minds discuss people." -Anonymous

**100.** "The mind is like an umbrella - it only works when it is open." - James Jeans

**101.** "Once you embrace unpleasant news not as a negative but as evidence of a need for change, you aren't defeated by it. You're learning from it." -Bill Gates

**102.** "Appreciation is a wonderful thing. It makes what is excellent in others belong to us as well." -Francois-Marie Arouet

**103.** "Comment is free, but facts are sacred." -C.P. Scott

**104.** "Learn from the mistakes of others. You can't live long enough to make them all yourself." -Eleanor Roosevelt

**105.** "Life can only be understood backwards; but it must be lived forwards." -Søren Kierkegaard

**106.** "The most subversive people are those who ask questions." - JosteinGaarder

**107.** "No government can now rely on the ignorance of its population to sustain it. We are richer as citizens thanks to the expansion of modern media." -White Paper

Rajeev Nair/flickr
http://www.flickr.com/photos/38523933@N00/377595734/in/photolist

108. "Discovery consists of seeing what everyone else has seen and thinking what no one else has thought." -Albert Szent-Gyorgyi

109. "All the masterpieces of art contain both light and shadow. A happy life is not one filled with only sunshine, but one which uses both light and shadow to produce beauty." -Billy Graham

110. "It is not things in themselves that trouble us but our opinion of things."-Epictetus

111. "A wise man proportions his belief to the evidence." -David Hulme

112. "Honest criticism is hard to take, particularly from a relative, a friend, an acquaintance or a stranger." -Franklin P Jones

113. "Too bad that all the people who know how to run the country are busy driving taxicabs and cutting hair."-George Burns

114. "Nobody made a greater mistake than he who did nothing because he could only do a little." -Edmund Burke

115. "The most important moment in your life is this one - right now. Truly it's the only moment that you have. All other moments are either over and are now just a memory or they are yet to be - a mere speculative thought about some future moment." -Richard Carlson

116. "I have made a ceaseless effort not to ridicule, not to bewail, not to scorn human actions, but to understand them." -Baruch Spinoza

117. "Anger is only one letter short of danger." -Anonymous

118. "Thinking is skilled work. It is not true that we are naturally endowed with the ability to think clearly and logically - without learning how or without practicing." -Alfred Mander

119. "It is better to have lived one day as a tiger than 1000 years as a sheep." -Tibetan proverb

120. "First they came for the socialists and I did not speak out because I was not a socialist. Then they came for the trade unionists and I did not speak out because I was not a trade unionist. Then they came for the Jews and I did not speak out because I was not a Jew. Then they came for me and there was no one left to speak for me." -Martin Niemöller

121. "The holes in your Swiss cheese are somebody else's Swiss cheese." -Melvin Fishman

122. "I find myself increasingly shocked at the unthinking and automatic rubbishing of men which is now so part of our culture that it is hardly even noticed." -Doris Lessing

123. "You cannot milk a cow with your hands in your pockets." - Russian proverb

124. "The greatest danger for most of us is not that our aim is too high and we miss it, but that it is too low and we reach it." - Buonarroti Michelangelo

125. "You would think the fury of aerial bombardment
Would rouse God to relent; the infinite spaces
Are still silent. He looks on shock-pried faces.
History, even, does not know what is meant." -Richard Eberhart

126. "All of us were born for one another."-Marcus Aurelius

127. "The ultimate measure of a man is not where he stands in moments of comfort and convenience, but where he stands at times of challenge and controversy."-Martin Luther King

128. "This is a moment to seize. The kaleidoscope has been shaken. The pieces are in flux. Soon they will settle again. Before they do, let us reorder this world around us." -Tony Blair

129. "If McWorld in its most elemental negative form is a kind of animal greed - one that is achieved by an aggressive and irresistible energy, Jihad in its most elemental negative form is a kind of animal fear propelled by anxiety in the face of uncertainty and relieved by self-sacrificing zealotry - an escape out of history." –McWorld

130. "There are no facts, only interpretations." -Friedrich Nietzsche

131. "The philosophers have only interpreted the world, in various ways; the point is to change it." -Karl Marx

132. "I wanted to change the world - but I found that the only thing one can be sure of changing is oneself." -Aldous Huxley

133. "Much research suggests that the language most likely to dominate the Internet in future years will be Chinese." -Henry Manisty

134. "You cannot hope to build a better world without improving the individual. To that end, each of us must work for his own improvement and, at the same time, share a general responsibility for all humanity." -Marie Curie

135. "Yesterday is history. Tomorrow is mystery. Today is a gift. That's why it's called the present." -Eleanor Roosevelt

136. "At each moment of life, you are at a fork in the road and you will choose which direction to take." -Richard Carlson

137. "Hold fast to dreams,
For if dreams die
Life is a broken-winged bird,
That cannot fly." -Langston Hughes

138. "The discipline of writing something down is the first step towards making it happen." -Lee Iacocca

139. "Learn to love change. If you appreciate that as much good comes from change as bad, you will avoid the concerns that many people seem to have about it. Relax and be open to change when it visits." -Paul Wilson

140. "Democratic and responsible trade unionism is the most powerful force for democracy and social justice around the world." -Denis MacShane

John Luker/flickr
http://www.flickr.com/photos/36860147@N06/3394643705/in/photolist

141. "The only thing necessary for the triumph of evil is for good men to do nothing." -Edmund Burke

142. "Now and then the workers are victorious, but only for a time. The real fruit of their battles lies, not in the immediate result, but in the ever-expanding union of the workers. This union is helped by the improved means of communication that are created by modern industry and that place the workers of different localities in contact with one another." -Karl Marx

143. "Today is the tomorrow that you worried about yesterday." - Anonymous

144. "What lies behind us and what lies before us are tiny matters compared to what lies within us." -Ralph Waldo Emerson

145. "Perfection of means and confusion of goals seem, in my opinion, to characterize our age." -Albert Einstein

146. "Without the bitter, baby, the sweet ain't as sweet." -Vanilla Sky

147. "Discard hard and fast rules. Victory is the only thing that matters and this cannot be achieved by adhering to conventional canons." -Sun-tzu

148. "The beautiful thing about learning is that nobody can take it away from you." -B B King

149. "That which does not defeat me makes me stronger." -Friedrich Nietzsche

150. "Life is just one damned thing after another." -Elbert Hubbard

151. "Many people will walk in and out of your life, but only true friends will leave footprints in your heart." -Eleanor Roosevelt

152. "Think, think, think. It will hurt like hell at first, but you'll get used to it." -Barbara Castle

153. "There's not much use in trying", said Alice. "One can't believe impossible things". "I dare say that you haven't had much practice", said the Queen. "Why sometimes, I've believed as many as six impossible things before breakfast."-Lewis Carroll

154. "Nothing great was ever achieved without enthusiasm." -Ralph Waldo Emerson

155. "The dreamers of the day are dangerous men, for they may act out their dream with open eyes, to make it possible." -T.E. Lawrence

156. "Until one is committed, there is hesitancy, the chance to draw back, always ineffectiveness. Concerning all acts of initiative, there is one elementary truth, the ignorance of which kills countless ideas and endless plans. That the moment one definitely commits oneself, then providence moves too. All sorts of things occur to help one that would never otherwise have occurred. A whole stream of events issue from the decision, raising in one's favor all manner of unforeseen incidents and meetings and material assistance which no man could have dreamed would come his way. Whatever you can do, or dream you can, begin it. Boldness has genius, power and magic in it. Begin it now!"-Johann Wolfgang von Goethe

157. "There was a time I used to reject those who were not of my faith. Now my heart has grown capable of taking on many forms: a pasture for gazelles, a convent for Christians, a temple for idols, a Kaaba for the pilgrim, a table for the Torah, a book of the Koran. My religion is love - whichever the route love's caravan shall take, that path shall be the path of my faith." -MuhyiddinIbn 'Arabi

158. "Education ends with death. Or after, according to your beliefs." -Peter Ustinov

159. "Confusion is the beginning of wisdom." Socrates

160. "Keep away from small people who try to belittle your ambitions. Small people always do that, but the really great make you feel that you, too, can become great." Mark Twain

161. "What is this life if, full of care,
we have no time to stand and stare?"-William Henry Davies

162. "We must learn to live together as brothers or perish together as fools."-Martin Luther King

163. "The wisest men follow their own direction and listen to no prophet guiding them."-Euripides

164. "Great opportunities to help others seldom come, but small ones surround us daily."-Sally Koch

165. "If we do not change direction, we may end up at the point at which we are heading."-Old Chinese proverb

166. "If at first an idea doesn't seem crazy, then there is no hope for it."-Scientist Albert Einstein

167. "There is nothing either good or bad, but thinking makes it so."-William Shakespeare

168. "It is in our idleness, in our dreams, that the submerged truth sometimes comes to the top."-Virginia Woolf

169. "They must often change who would be constant in happiness or wisdom."-Confucius

Randy Robertson/flickr
http://www.flickr.com/photos/46042146@N00/2134087952/in/photolist

170. "Cowardice asks the question - is it safe? Expediency asks the question - is it politic? Vanity asks the question - is it popular? But conscience asks the question - is it right? There comes a time when one must take a position that is neither safe, nor politic, nor popular; but one must take it because it is right." - Martin Luther King

171. "The greatest good you can do for another is not just share your riches, but to reveal to him his own." -Benjamin Disraeli

172. "They that can give up essential liberty to obtain a little temporary safety deserve neither liberty nor safety." -Benjamin Franklin

173. "Experience is not what happens to a man; it is what a man does with what happens to him." -Aldous Huxley

174. "Exhaust the little moment. Soon it dies. And be it gash or gold it will not come again in this identical disguise." -Gwendolyn Brooks

175. "Things which matter most must never be at the mercy of things which matter least." -Johann Wolfgang von Goethe

176. "Twenty years from now, you will be more disappointed by the things you didn't do, than by the ones you did. So throw off the bowlines. Sail away from the safe harbor. Catch the trade winds in your sails. Explore. Dream. Discover" -Mark Twain

177. "There is only one thing in the world worse than being talked about and that is not being talked about." -Oscar Wilde

178. "Politics is what we create by what we do, what we hope for and what we dare to imagine." -Paul Wellstone

179. "I am in the world to change the world." -Käthe Kollwitz

180. "There is only one thing that makes a dream impossible to achieve: the fear of failure." -Paulo Coelho

181. "He who does not ask a question learns nothing." -Swahili proverb

182. "Nobody grows old merely by living a number of years. We grow old by deserting our ideals. Years may wrinkle the skin, but to give up enthusiasm wrinkles the soul." -Samuel Ullman

183. "Our deepest fear is not that we are inadequate. Our deepest fear is that we are powerful beyond measure. It is our light, not our darkness, that most frightens us. We ask ourselves: 'Who am I to be brilliant, gorgeous, talented and fabulous?' Actually, who are you not to be?" -Nelson Mandela

184. "We always overestimate the change that will occur in the next two years and underestimate the change that will occur in the next ten." -Bill Gates

185. "If you can dream - and not make dreams your master;
If you can think - and not make thought your aim;
If you can meet with triumph and disaster
And treat those two impostors just the same ...." -Rudyard Kipling

186. "You make a choice or set a goal and let people know about it. Then just getting started leads to the discovery of internal resources that help us to go further than we ever thought we could."-Christopher Reeve

187. "It is not our abilities that truly define us - it is the choices we make." -J K Rowling

188. "When you were born, you were crying and everyone around you was smiling. Live your life so that, when you die, you're the one who is smiling and everyone around you is crying."-Anonymous

189. "Brevity is the sister of talent." -Anton Chekhov

190. "If all the world valued food and merriment above mountains of treasure, the earth would be a happier place." -J R R Tolkien

191. "To be truly radical is to make hope possible rather than despair convincing."-Raymond Williams

192. "If you no got smile on you face, no use open shop."-Jamaican proverb

193. "Don't agonize, organize."-Florynce Kennedy

194. "When I do good, I feel good. When I do bad, I feel bad. And that's my religion." -Abraham Lincoln

195. "It is not the critic who counts: not the man who points out how the strong man stumbles or where the doer of deeds could have done better. The credit belongs to the man who is actually in the arena, whose face is marred by dust and sweat and blood, who strives valiantly, who errs and comes up short again and again." -Theodore Roosevelt

196. "You have to take chances for peace, just as you must take chances in war." -John Foster Dulles

197. "Critical thinking should center not on answering questions but on questioning answers." -Sonia Livingstone

198. "So many of our dreams at first seem impossible, then they seem improbable, and then, when we summon the will, they soon become inevitable." -Christopher Reeve

199. "Our prime purpose in this life is to help others. And if you can't help them, at least don't hurt them." -Dalai Lama

200. "Don't say you don't have enough time. You have the same number of hours per day as Helen Keller, Pasteur, Michelangelo, Mother Teresa, Leonardo da Vinci, Thomas Jefferson and Albert Einstein." -H. Jackson Brown Jr

201. "No matter what he does, every person on earth plays a central role in the history of the world. And normally he doesn't know it." -Paulo Coelho

202. "Make new friends
but keep the old.
One is silver
and the other is gold." -Anonymous

203. "It is good to have an end to journey towards, but it is the journey that matters in the end."-Ursula Le Guin

204. "Hold yourself responsible for a higher standard than anybody else expects of you. Never excuse yourself. Never pity yourself. Be a hard master to yourself - and be lenient to everybody else."-Henry Ward Beecher

205. "Now and then it's good to pause in our pursuit of happiness and just be happy."-Guillaume Apollinaire

206. "If the earth's life were seen as a single day, human beings proper would only appear in the last second before midnight."-Chris Brazier

207. "Into the hands of every individual is given a marvelous power for good or evil - the silent, unconscious, unseen influence of his life. This is simply the constant radiation of what man really is, not what he pretends to be."-William George Jordan

208. "We live by encouragement and die without it - slowly, sadly, angrily."-Celeste Holm

209. "Your time has a limit set to it. Use it, then to advance your enlightenment; or it will be gone and never in your power again."-Marcus Aurelius

210. "A new broom sweeps clean, but an old one knows all the corners."-Jamaican proverb

211. "Never look down on anybody unless you're helping them up."-Jesse Jackson

Jonah Sharkey/flickr
http://www.flickr.com/photos/71002359@N00/2937599751/in/photolist

212. "If we don't do the impossible, we shall be faced with the unthinkable." -Petra Kelly

213. "I arise in the morning torn between a desire to improve (or save) the world and a desire to enjoy (or savor) the world. This makes it hard to plan the day." -Elwyn Brooks White

214. "There is a difference between knowledge and wisdom. Knowledge is knowing that a tomato is a fruit not a vegetable. Wisdom is knowing not to include it in a fruit salad."-Anonymous

215. "Rest satisfied with doing well and leave others to talk of you as they will."-Pythagoras

216. "If you obey all the rules, you miss all the fun."-Katherine Hepburn

217. "A person without a sense of humor is like a wagon without springs, jolted by every pebble in the road."-Henry Ward Beecher

218. "Wealth, if you use it, comes to an end; learning, if you use it, increases."-Swahili proverb

219. "The means by which we live have outdistanced the ends for which we live. Our scientific power has outrun our spiritual power. We have guided missiles but misguided men."-Martin Luther King

220. "The biggest room in the world is the room for improvement."-Chris Eubank

221. "The world can only be grasped by action, not by contemplation. The hand is the cutting edge of the mind."-Jacob Bronowski

222. "Never be afraid to tread the path alone. Know which is your path and follow it wherever it may lead you. Do not feel you have to follow is someone else's footsteps." Eileen Caddy

223. "A little rebellion now and then is a good thing."-Thomas Jefferson

224. "He who awaits much can expect little."-Gabriel Garcia Marquez

225. "Success is a journey, not a destination - half the fun is getting there." Gita Bellin

226. "Life isn't about finding yourself. Life is about creating yourself."-George Bernard Shaw

227. "Ask yourself this daily question: 'How would the person I'd like to be ... do the things I'm about to do?"-Jim Cathcart

228. "You can blame people who knock things over in the dark, or you can begin to light candles. You're only at fault if you know about the problem and choose to do nothing."-Paul Hawken

229. "It is necessary to write, if the days are not to slip emptily by. How else, indeed, to clap the net over the butterfly of the moment?"-Vita Sackville-West

230. "Three things cannot long be hidden: the sun, the moon, and the truth."-Confucius

231. "When everyone agrees, someone is not thinking."-George S. Patton

232. "No good act performed in the world ever dies. Science tells us that no atom of matter can ever be destroyed, that no force once started ever ends; it merely passes through a multiplicity

of ever-changing phases. Every good deed done to others is a great force that starts an unending pulsation through time and eternity. We may not know it, we may never hear a word of gratitude or recognition, but it will all come back to us in some form as naturally, as perfectly, as inevitably, as echo answers to sound."-William George Jordan

233. "This is what learning is. You suddenly understand something you've understood all your life, but in a new way."-Doris Lessing

234. "Hope is an orientation of the heart; it transcends the world that is immediately experienced and it is anchored somewhere beyond its horizons. It is an ability to work for something because it is good, not just because it stands a chance to succeed."-Vaclav Havel

Enokson/flickr

235. "Not all those who wander are lost."-J R R Tolkien

236. "There is no guarantee of reaching a goal at a certain time, but there is a guarantee of never attaining goals that are never set."-David McNally

237. "Dream as though you'll live for ever; live as though you'll die today." -James Dean

238. "The love of one's country is a splendid thing. But why should love stop at the border?" -Pablo Casals

239. "Before I can live with other folks I've got to live with myself. The one thing that doesn't abide by majority rule is a person's conscience."-Harper Lee

240. "Imagination is more important than knowledge." -Albert Einstein

241. "Nothing contributes so much to tranquillize the mind as a steady purpose - a point on which the soul may fix its intellectual eye." -Wollstonecraft Shelley

242. "People will not always remember what you said. People will not always remember what you did. But people will always remember how you made them feel."-Anonymous

243. "Don't tell people how to do things. Tell them what to do and let them surprise you with their results."-George S. Patton

244. "Believe, no pessimist ever discovered the secrets of the stars, or sailed to an uncharted land, or opened a new heaven to the human spirit."-Helen Keller

245. "Opportunity dances with those who are already on the dance floor."-H. Jackson Brown Jr.

246. "The Chinese use two brush strokes to write the word 'crisis.' One brush stroke stands for danger; the other for opportunity. In a crisis, be aware of the danger - but recognize the opportunity."-John F Kennedy

247. "The greatest mistake you can make in life is to be continually fearing you will make one."-Elbert Hubbard

248. "Friendship is unnecessary, like philosophy, like art. It has no survival value; rather it is one of those things that give value to survival."-C S Lewis

249. "The difference between perseverance and obstinacy is that one often comes from a strong will, and the other from a strong won't."-Henry Ward Beecher

250. "In every field of endeavor, there are the timid and there are the tigers. Go on. Be a tiger."-Accenture

251. "All rising to a great place is by a winding stair."-Francis Bacon

252. "Squeeze the past like a sponge, smell the present like a rose, and send a kiss to the future."-Arabic proverb

253. "It is harder to crack a prejudice than an atom."-Albert Einstein

254. "A good plan, violently executed now, is better than a perfect plan next week."-George S Patton

255. "It is one of the most beautiful compensations of life, that no man can sincerely try to help another without helping himself."-Ralph Waldo Emerson

256. "Everything has beauty, but not everyone sees it."-Confucius

257. "Every time we say 'I must do something' it takes an incredible amount of energy. Far more than physically doing it."-Gita Bellin

258. "Simply seek happiness and you are not likely to find it. Seek to create and love without regard to your happiness and you are likely to be happy much of the time."-M Scott Peck

259. "The best thing about the future is that it comes only one day at a time."-Abraham Lincoln

260. "Blessed is he who expects nothing, for he shall never be disappointed."- Alexander Pope

261. "Humility does not mean you think less of yourself. It means you think of yourself less."-Dr Kenneth Blanchard

262. "Perhaps it is better to be irresponsible and right than to be responsible and wrong."-Winston Churchill

263. "We shall not cease from exploration
And the end of all our exploring
Will be to arrive where we started
And know the place for the first time."-T.S. Eliot

264. "Life shrinks or expands in proportion to one's courage."-Anais Nin

265. "If things do not turn out as we wish, we should wish for them as they turn out."-Aristotle

266. "A man should never be ashamed to own he has been wrong, which is but saying, that he is wiser today than he was yesterday."-Alexander Pope

267. "It's never too late to have a happy childhood."-Tom Robbins

268. "Sow a thought, reap a deed; sow a deed, reap a habit; sow a habit, reap a lifestyle; sow a lifestyle, reap a destiny."-Charles Reed

269. "You cannot plough a field by turning it over in your mind."-Anonymous

270. "Daring ideas are like chessmen moved forward; they may be beaten, but they may start a winning game."-Johann Wolfgang

271. "We don't see things as they are, we see them as we are."-Anais Nin

272. "If you are going through hell, keep going."-Winston Churchill

273. "Man cannot discover new oceans unless he has the courage to lose sight of the shore."-André Gide

**274.** "Music is medicine to man."-Mary's Church

Lisa Birtch/flickr
http://www.flickr.com/photos/24172622@N04/3208139308/in/photolist

**275.** "In this media-drenched, data-rich, channel-surfing, computer-gaming age, we have lost the art of doing nothing, of shutting out the background noise and distractions, of slowing down and simply being alone with our thoughts." -Carl Honoré

**276.** "A friend is a present you give yourself."-Robert Louis Stevenson

**277.** "We have to be all those difficult things like cheerful and kind and curious and brave and patient; and we've got to study and think, and work hard, all of us, in all our different worlds."-Philip Pullman

**278.** "Choose a job you love and you will never have to work a day in your life." -Confucius

279. "The spirit of Ubuntu* - that profound African sense that we are human beings only through the humanity of other human beings - is not a parochial phenomenon, but has added globally to our common search for a better world."-Nelson Mandela

280. "Much madness is divinest sense
To a discerning eye;
Much sense the starkest madness." -Emily Dickenson

281. "We all do better when we work together. Our differences do matter, but our common humanity matters more." -Bill Clinton

282. "A pessimist sees the difficulty in every opportunity; an optimist sees the opportunity in every difficulty." -Winston Churchill

283. "Even a happy life cannot be without a measure of darkness and the word happy would lose its meaning if it were not balanced by sadness." -Carl Jung

284. "A thing of beauty is a joy forever." -John Keats

285. "The best way to cheer yourself up is to try to cheer somebody else up."-Mark Twain

286. "Each friend represents a world in us, a world possibly not born until they arrive, and it is only by this meeting that a new world is born." -Anais Nin

287. "When one door closes another door opens; but we so often look so long and so regretfully upon the closed door, that we do not see the ones which open for us." -Alexander Graham Bell

288. "The cruelest lies are often told in silence." -Adlai Stevenson

289. "The world is a book and those who do not travel read only a page." -Saint Augustine

290. "The greatest and most important problems of life are all fundamentally insoluble. They can never be solved but only outgrown." -Carl Jung

291. "No one is born hating another person because of the color of his skin, or his background, or his religion. People must learn to hate, and if they can learn to hate, they can be taught to love, for love comes more naturally to the human heart than its opposite." -Nelson Mandela

292. "Without music, life would be a mistake."-Friedrich Wilhelm Nietzsche

293. "Money is like manure - it should be spread around." -Christo

294. "The really happy person is the one who can enjoy the scenery, even when they have to take a detour."-James Hopwood Jeans

295. "Better light a candle than curse the darkness." -Chinese proverb

296. "The totality of life, known as the biosphere to scientists and creation to theologians, is a membrane of organisms wrapped around Earth so thin that it cannot be seen edgewise from a space shuttle, yet so internally complex that most species composing it remain undiscovered." -E.O. Wilson

297. "The happiest of people don't necessarily have the best of everything; they just make the most of everything that comes along their way." -Anonymous

298. "We have in our hands the power and obligation - never given to any other generation at any other time in human history - to banish ignorance and poverty from the earth." -Gordon Brown

299. "Life is not measured by the breaths we take but by the moments that take our breath away." -Will Smith

300. "Not everything that counts can be counted and not everything that can be counted counts."-Albert Einstein

301. "We are different so that we know our need of one another, for no one is ultimately self-sufficient. A completely self-sufficient person would be sub-human." -Desmond Tutu

302. "Freedom for the pike is death to the minnow." -Isaiah Berlin

**303.** "Everything changes. We plant trees for those born later." - Cicely Herbert

**304.** "We ought not to be ashamed of applauding the truth, nor appropriating the truth, from whatever source it may come, even if it be from remote races and nations alien to us."-Al-Kindi

**305.** "Man's goodness is a flame that can be hidden but never extinguished." -Nelson Mandela

Jonny Hughes/flickr
http://www.flickr.com/photos/23823986@N05/4208794068/in/photolist

**306.** "You must be the change you wish to see in the world." -Mahatma Gandhi

**307.** "An inch of time is an inch of gold, but you can't buy that inch of time with an inch of gold." -Chinese proverb

**308.** "We must never forget that we may also find meaning in life even when confronted with a hopeless situation, when facing a fate that cannot be changed. When we are no longer able to change a situation…we are challenged to change ourselves."-Viktor E Frankl

**309.** "Those who cannot remember the past are condemned to repeat it." -George Santayana

**310.** "Learning without thought is labor lost; thought without learning is perilous." -Confucious

**311.** "Don't let one cloud obliterate the whole sky."-Anais Nin

**312.** "Who struggles can fail. Who doesn't struggle has already failed." -Berthold Brecht

**313.** "I don't feel the least humble before the vastness of the heavens. The stars may be large, but they cannot think or love."-F.P. Ramsey

**314.** "The man who removes a mountain begins by carrying away small stones."-Chinese proverb

315. "There are few misfortunes in this world that you cannot turn into a personal triumph if you have the iron will and the necessary skill."-Nelson Mandela

316. "If nothing ever changed, there'd be no butterflies."-Anonymous

317. "Why do we fall? So that we might better learn to pick ourselves up."-Batman Begins

318. "The sleep of reason brings forth monsters."-Francis Wheen

319. "When I look back on all these worries, I remember the story of the old man who said on his deathbed that he had had a lot of troubles in his life, most of which had never happened." Winston Churchill

320. "What do we live for, if it is not to make life less difficult for each other?"-George Eliot

321. "Lose your temper and you lose a friend; lie and you lose yourself."-Hopi proverb

322. "I am only one, but still I am one. I cannot do everything, but still I can do something; and because I cannot do everything, I will not refuse to do something that I can do."-Helen Keller

323. "Some people take no mental exercise apart from jumping to conclusions."-Harold Acton

324. "Women are half the world's people who do two-thirds of the world's work. They earn a tenth of the world's income and own a hundredth of the world's property." -WomenAid International

325. "When a finger points at the moon, the fool looks at the finger."-Chinese proverb

326. "We must use time wisely and forever realize that the time is always ripe to do right."-Nelson Mandela

327. "I keep six honest serving-men
(They taught me all I knew);
Their names are What and Why and When
And How and Where and Who."-Rudyard Kipling

328. "If you are patient in one moment of anger, you will escape a hundred days of sorrow."-Chinese proverb

329. "All endings are also beginnings. We just don't know it at the time."-Mitch Albom

330. "In this very real world, good doesn't drive out evil. Evil doesn't drive out good. But the energetic displaces the passive."-William Bernbach

331. 'Those of us enjoying freedom and with our basic needs met, have a moral obligation to engage in compassionate activism on behalf of those who have no freedom, who have no voice,

whose situation is precarious, whose lives are in crisis." -Pida Ripley

332. "You may be only one person in the world, but you may also be the world to one person." -Anonymous

333. "Mother Earth is not a resource; she is an heirloom." -David Ipinia

334. "An idea can turn to dust or magic, depending on the talent that rubs against it." -William Bernbach

335. "The important work of moving the world forward does not wait to be done by perfect men." -Mary Ann Evans

336. "The person who says it can't be done should not interrupt the person doing it." -Chinese proverb

337. "Patriotism is not enough. I must have no hatred or bitterness for anyone."-Edith Cavell

338. "Good advice is better than gold." Czech proverb

339. "When the facts change, I change my mind."-John Maynard Keynes

340. "The real voyage of discovery begins not in seeking new landscapes, but in having new eyes." -Marcel Proust

341. "God gave man two ears but only one mouth that he might hear twice as much as he speaks." -Epictetus

342. "Failing to prepare is preparing to fail." -Anonymous

343. "It's never too late to be who you might have been." -George Eliot

344. "Lost time never returns." -Czech proverb

345. "If a free society cannot help the many who are poor, it cannot save the the few who are rich." -John F Kennedy

346. "An inability to stay quiet is one of the conspicuous failings of mankind." -Walter Bagehot

347. "To utter pleasant words without practicing them is like a fine flower without fragrance." —Buddha

348. "The key to success is to risk thinking unconventional thoughts." -Trevor Baylis

349. "Always wear a smile. The gift of life will then be yours to give." -Rabbi Nachman

350. "You have to find what's good and true and beautiful in your life as it is now." -Mitch Albom

351. "I look forward to seeing more and more people willing to resist the direction the world is moving in: a direction where our personal experiences are irrelevant, that we are defective, that our communities are not important, that we are powerless, that the future is determined, and that the highest level of humanity is expressed through what we choose to buy at the mall." -Rachel Corrie

352. "Thinking is not entertainment but an obligation." -ArkadyNatanovichStrugatsky

353. "Love is the only rational act."-Stephen Levine

354. "Data, data everywhere, but never time to think."-Sonia Livingstone

355. "Happy thoughts are half your health."-Czech proverb

356. "A problem well stated is a problem half solved."-Charles Kettering

357. "Worry does not empty tomorrow of its sorrow; it empties today of its strength."-Holocaust Corrie

358. "The best time to plant a tree is 20 years ago. The second best is now."-Chinese proverb

359. "Do what gives you a buzz."-Trevor Baylis

Oscar E./flickr
http://www.flickr.com/photos/skateimpulse/2328304838/

360. "We all should know that diversity makes for a rich tapestry, and we must understand that all the threads of the tapestry are equal in value no matter what their color."-Maya Angelou

361. "You can't substitute material things for love or for gentleness or for tenderness or for a sense of comradeship." -Mitch Albom

362. "Courage doesn't always roar. Sometimes courage is the quiet voice at the end of the day saying, 'I will try again tomorrow." -Mary Anne Radmacher

363. "Have patience. All things change in due time. Wishing cannot bring autumn glory or cause winter to cease." -Cherokee Ginaly-li

364. "Love each other or perish." -W H Auden

365. "He who laughs, lasts." -Mary Pettibone Poole

366. "Each night, when I go to sleep, I die. And the next morning, when I wake up, I am reborn." -Mahatma Gandhi

367. "Do what you can, with what you have, where you are."-Eleanor Roosevelt

368. "People who care about other people are on average happier than those who are more preoccupied with themselves." -Richard Layard

369. "Although the world is full of suffering, it is also full of the overcoming of it."-Helen Keller

370. "Of all forms of caution, caution in love is the most fatal to true happiness."-Bertrand Russell

371. "I know for sure that what we dwell on is what we become."-Oprah Winfrey

372. "There is no such thing as 'too late' in life."-Mitch Albom

373. "We live in an age of unprecedented change."-Adam to Eve

374. "Wisdom consists not so much in knowing what to do in the ultimate as in knowing what to do next."-Herbert Hoover

375. "If you sow the seed of good, it will grow into seven ears and then yield seven hundred good deeds."-Mohammed BakhauddinNakhshbandi

376. "Friends are the family we choose for ourselves."-Edna Buchanan

377. "No one is useless in the world who lightens the burdens of another."-Charles Dickens

378. "Only dead fish swim with the tide."-Trevor Baylis

379. "The gem cannot be polished without friction, nor man perfected without trials."-Chinese proverb

380. "It is not necessary to change. Survival is not mandatory."-W. Edwards Deming

381. "There are four things that hold back human progress: ignorance, stupidity, committees and accountants."-Charles James Lyall

382. "Wonder is the beginning of wisdom."-Greek proverb

383. "Live out of your imagination, not your history."-Stephen Covey

384. "It is from ignorance and greed that the world of delusion is born and the vast complexity of coordinating causes exists within the mind and nowhere else."-Buddha

385. "A kind word warms for three winters."-Chinese proverb

386. "A bad word whispered will echo a hundred miles."-Chinese proverb

387. "The seven blunders that human society commits and cause all the violence: wealth without work, pleasure without conscience, knowledge without character, commerce without morality, science without humanity, worship without sacrifice, and politics without principles."-Mahatma Gandhi

388. "Remember that there is nothing stable in human affairs; therefore avoid undue elation in prosperity or undue depression in adversity."-Socrates

389. "Be who you are and say what you feel, because those who mind don't matter and those who matter don't mind."-Theodor Seuss Geisel

390. "Man holds in his mortal hands the power to abolish all forms of human poverty and all forms of human life."-John F Kennedy

391. "Not to know is bad, but not to wish to know is worse."-West African proverb

392. "Strange is our situation here on Earth. Each of us comes for a short visit, not knowing why, yet sometimes seeming to divine a purpose. From the standpoint of our daily life, however, there is one thing we do know: that man is here for the sake of other men - above all for those upon whose smiles and well-being our own happiness depends."-Albert Einstein

393. "Behold the turtle. He makes progress only when he sticks his neck out."-James Bryant Conant

394. "A half truth is a whole lie."-Yiddish proverb

395. "Whether you think you can or think you can't, you're probably right."-Henry Ford

396. "He is a wise man who does not grieve for the things which he has not, but rejoices for those which he has."-Epictetus

397. "A ship is safe in harbor, but that's not what ships are for."-William Shedd

398. "Remember, no one can make you feel inferior without your consent."-Eleanor Roosevelt

399. "The mystery of life isn't a problem to solve, but a reality to experience."-Frank Herbert

**400.** "Our true nationality is mankind."-H. G. Wells

**401.** "The most beautiful thing under the sun is being under the sun."-Christa Wolf

**402.** "Of all the things that wisdom provides to help one live one's life in happiness, the greatest by far is friendship."-Epicurus

**403.** "Commandment Number One of any truly civilized society is this: let people be different."-David Grayson

**404.** "To attract good fortune, spend a new coin on an old friend, share an old pleasure with a new friend, and lift up the heart of a true friend by writing his name on the wings of a dragon."-Chinese proverb

**405.** "Life is the greatest bargain - we get it for nothing."-Yiddish proverb

**406.** "The fact that we live at the bottom of a deep gravity well, on the surface of a gas-covered planet, going around a nuclear fireball ninety million miles away and think this is normal is obviously some indication of how skewed our perspective tends to be."-Douglas Adams

**407.** "We are the hero of our own story."-Mary McCarthy

**408.** "The truth of the matter is that you always know the right thing to do. The hard part is doing it."-Schwarzkopf

**409.** "Patience is bitter, but its fruit is sweet."-Jean Jacques Rousseau

**410.** "Those who stand for nothing fall for anything."-Alex Hamilton

**411.** "Recognition is the greatest motivator."-Eakedale

**412.** "If you don't like something, change it. If you can't change it, change your attitude. Don't complain."-Maya Angelou

**413.** "A person is a person through other people."-Setswana proverb

**414.** "To accomplish great things, we must not only act, but also dream; not only plan, but also believe."-Anatole France

**415.** "By three methods we may learn wisdom: first, by reflection, which is noblest; second, by imitation, which is easiest; and third by experience, which is the bitterest."-Confucius

**416.** "All government, indeed every human benefit and enjoyment, every virtue, and every prudent act, is founded on compromise and barter."-Edmund Burke

**417.** "The best way to have a good idea is to have lots of ideas."-Linus Pauling

418. "Treat people as if they were what they ought to be, and you help them to become what they are capable of being."-Johann Wolfgang

419. "Your assumptions are your windows on the world. Scrub them off every once in a while, or the light won't come in."-Alan Alda

420. "Some people bear three kinds of trouble - the ones they've had, the ones they have, and the ones they expect to have."-H. G. Wells

421. "The range of sizes, distances or speeds with which our imaginations are comfortable is a tiny band, set in the midst of a gigantic range of the possible, from the scale of quantum strangeness at the smaller end to the scale of Einsteinian cosmology at the larger."-Richard Dawkins

422. "In complete darkness we are all the same. It is only our knowledge and wisdom that separates us. Don't let your eyes deceive you."-Janet Jackson

423. "It is better to debate a question without settling it than to settle a question without debating it."- Joseph Joubert

424. "Life is like a pen, you can cross something out but you can never erase it."-Anonymous

**425.** "An eye for an eye only ends up making the whole world blind."-Mahatma Gandhi

**426.** "Happiness is a how, not a what; a talent, not an object."-Hermann Hesse

**427.** "Do not go where the path may lead; go instead where there is no path and leave a trail."-Ralph Waldo Emerson

**428.** "Man is a credulous animal and must believe something; in the absence of good grounds for belief, he will be satisfied with bad ones."-Bertrand Russell

Jan Tik/flickr
http://www.flickr.com/photos/15363357@N00/91151137/in/photolist

**429.** "A stumble may prevent a fall."-English proverb

430. "Make all you can; save all you can; give all you can."-John Wesley

431. "To teach is to learn twice."-Joseph Joubert

432. "Finish each day and be done with it. You have done what you could."-Ralph Waldo Emerson

433. "You can always learn something from somebody."-Rafael Benitez

434. "For to be free is not to merely cast off one's chains, but to live in a way that respects and enhances the freedom of others."-Nelson Mandela

435. "Happiness and laughter - that's what it's all about, isn't it?"-Peggy Clark

436. "The great mistakes are made when we feel we are beyond questioning."-William Bernbach

437. "The sleep of reason breeds monsters."-Francisco de Goya

438. "Everything that ever happens in life has an end as well as a beginning."-Tonga proverb

439. "Don't walk in front of me, I may not follow; don't walk behind me, I may not lead; walk beside me, and just be my friend."-Albert Camus

440. "What sunshine is to flowers, smiles are to humanity. They are but trifles to be sure, but the good they do is inconceivable."-Joseph Addison

441. "Dreams, dreams, without dreams man is a bird without wings."-Sergei Korolev

442. "Always be a little kinder than necessary."-Chinese fortune cookie

443. "If you want to lift yourself up, lift up someone else."-Booker T. Washington

444. "Those who are at war with others are not at peace with themselves."-William Hazlitt

445. "What you leave behind is not what is engraved in stone monuments, but what is woven into the lives of others."-Pericles

446. "You begin saving the world by saving one person at a time."-Charles Bukowski

447. "If you stand for something, you will always find some people for you and some against you. If you stand for nothing, you will

find nobody against you, and nobody for you."-William Bernbach

448. "If you wish success in life, make perseverance your bosom friend, experience your wise counsellor, caution your elder brother, and hope your guardian genius."-Joseph Addison

449. "I can live for two months on a good compliment."-Mark Twain

450. "Even after all this time
The sun never says to the earth,
'You owe me'.
Look what happens with a love like that...
it lights the whole sky."-Hafez of Shiraz

451. "If you have zest and enthusiasm, you attract zest and enthusiasm. Life does give back in kind."-Vincent Peale

452. "No act of kindness, however small, is ever wasted."-Aesop

453. "You can't control the wind, but you can adjust your sails."-Yiddish proverb

454. "The greatest prize that life has to offer is the chance to do hard work that is worth doing."-Theodore Roosevelt

455. "Be true to your work, your word, and your friend."-Henry David Thoreau

456. "One-fifth of the people are against everything all of the time."-Robert F Kennedy

457. "The ideals which have lighted me on my way and time after time given me new courage to face life cheerfully, have been truth, goodness, and beauty. The ordinary objects of human endeavor - property, outward success, luxury - have always seemed to me contemptible."-Albert Einstein

458. "Remember - a statue has never been set up in honor of a critic."-Jean Sibelius

459. "If it is not right, do not do it; if it is not true, do not say it."-Marcus Aurelius

460. "To live for only some future goal is shallow. It's the sides of the mountain that sustain life, not the top."-Robert Pirsig

461. "Washing one's hands of the conflict between the powerful and the powerless means to side with the powerful, not to be neutral."-Paulo Freire

462. "The world is too dangerous for anything but truth and too small for anything but love."-Clergyman William Sloane Coffin

463. "Far better is it to dare mighty things, to win glorious triumphs even though checkered by failure than to take rank with those poor spirits who neither enjoy much nor suffer much because

they live in the grey twilight that knows neither victory nor defeat."-Theodore Roosevelt

464. "Never apologize for showing feeling. When you do so, you apologize for the truth."-Benjamin Disraeli

465. "Create all the happiness you are able to create; remove all the misery you are able to remove. Every day will allow you to add something to the pleasure of others, and to diminish something of their pains."-Jeremy Bentham

466. "You cannot stop the birds of sorrow from landing on your shoulder, but you can prevent them nesting in your hair."-Chinese proverb

467. "We do not need magic to change the world, we carry all the power we need inside ourselves already: we have the power to imagine better."-J.K. Rowling

468. "Our life is frittered away by detail. Simplify, simplify."-Henry David Thoreau

469. "The greatest part of our happiness depends on our dispositions, not our circumstances."-Martha Washington

470. "As is a tale, so is life: not how long it is, but how good it is, is what matters."-Seneca

QUOI Media Group/flickr
http://www.flickr.com/photos/49698777@N02/4923656324/in/photolist

**471.** "Nothing worthwhile was ever accomplished without the will to start, the enthusiasm to continue and, regardless of temporary obstacles, the persistence to complete."-Waite Phillips

**472.** "Though force can protect in emergency, only justice, fairness, consideration and cooperation can finally lead men to the dawn of eternal peace."-Dwight D. Eisenhower

**473.** "The difficult is what takes a little time; the impossible is what takes a little longer."-Norwegian Fridtjof Nansen

**474.** "Everyone is entitled to their own opinion, but not their own facts."-Daniel Patrick Moynihan

475. "Ever tried? Ever failed? No matter. Try again. Fail again. Fail better."-Samuel Beckett

476. "Do your little bit of good where you are; its those little bits of good put together that overwhelm the world."-Desmond Tutu

477. "You make a living by what you get, but you make a life by what you give."-Winston Churchill

478. "If you have made mistakes, even serious mistakes, you can make a new start whenever you choose. For the thing we call failure is not the falling but the staying down."-Mary Pickford

479. "Perhaps you will forget tomorrow the kind words you say today, but the recipient may cherish them over a lifetime."-Dale Carnegie

480. "In a time of universal deceit, telling the truth becomes a revolutionary act."-George Orwell

481. "If one advances confidently in the direction of his dreams, and endeavors to live the life which he has imagined, he will meet with a success unexpected in common hours."-Henry David Thoreau

482. "To be avoided at all costs is the solace of opinion without the pain of thought."-Clergyman William Sloane Coffin

483. "I don't mind if my future is long or short, as long as I'm doing the right thing."-Henry Allingham

484. "One of the symptoms of an approaching nervous breakdown is the belief that one's work is terribly important."-Bertrand Russell

485. "We judge others by their behavior, but ourselves by our intentions."-Stephen Covey

486. "After six years without seeing one, I love just seeing a smile - every smile I see gives me hope."-Ingrid Betancourt

487. "And in the end, it's not the years in your life that count. It's the life in your years."-Abraham Lincoln

488. "It is well to remember that the entire universe, with one trifling exception, is composed of others."-John Andrew Holmes

489. "For every grain of enjoyment you sow in the bosom of another, you shall find a harvest in your own bosom; while every sorrow which you pluck out from the thoughts and feelings of a fellow creature shall be replaced by beautiful peace and joy in the sanctuary of your soul."-Jeremy Bentham

490. "Between the optimist and the pessimist, the difference is droll. The optimist sees the doughnut; the pessimist the hole."-Oscar Wilde

491. "If we choose to focus our awareness and energy on those things and people that bring us pleasure and satisfaction, we

have a very good chance of being happy in a world full of unhappiness."-Gordon Livingston MD

492. "Do whatever you can, with whatever you have been given, in the time you have, wherever you are."-Nkosi Johnston

493. "I think you'll find it's a bit more complicated than that."- Ben Goldacre

494. "It's a rare gift to understand that your life is wondrous and that it won't last for ever."-Steven Galloway

495. "We are not what we think or what we say or what we feel. We are what we do."-Gordon Livingston MD

496. "The unexamined life is not worth living."-Socrates

497. "You will never truly know yourself, or the strength of your relationships, until both have been tested by adversity. Such knowledge is a true gift, for all that it is painfully won."-J.K. Rowling

498. "I can give you a six-word formula for success: 'Think things through - then follow through."-Edward Rickenbacker

499. "Life is a gamble in which we don't get to deal the cards, but are nevertheless obligated to play them to the best of our ability."-Gordon Livingston MD

**500.** "The demand for certainty is one which is natural to man, but is nevertheless an intellectual vice."-Bertrand Russell

**501.** "It is never too late to give up your prejudices."-Henry David Thoreau

Leland Francisco/flickr
http://www.flickr.com/photos/22779530@N02/5686513127/in/photolist

**502.** "I don't understand why people are scared of difference because difference is what makes life interesting."-Jarvis Cocker

**503.** "A crank is a small engine that causes revolutions."-Frank Sheehy-Skeffington

504. "People often tell me that motivation doesn't last, and I tell them that bathing doesn't either. That's why I recommend it daily."-Hilary Hinton

505. "The three components of happiness are something to do, someone to love, and something to look forward to."-Gordon Livingston

506. "You cannot open a book without learning something."-Confucius

507. "Even if you're on the right track, you'll get run over if you just sit there."-Will Rogers

508. "When someone hurts us, we should write it down in sand, where winds of forgiveness can erase it away. But, when someone does something good for us, we must engrave it in stone, where no wind can ever erase it."–Anonymous

509. "The process of learning consists not so much in accumulating answers as in figuring out how to formulate the right questions."-Gordon Livingston

510. "The trouble with the world is that the stupid are cocksure while the intelligent are full of doubt."-Bertrand Russell

511. "Under certain circumstances, there are few hours in life more agreeable than the hour dedicated to the ceremony known as afternoon tea."-Henry James

512. "If your actions inspire others to dream more, learn more, do more and become more, you are a leader."-John Quincy Adams

513. "What happens to us is not nearly as important as the attitude we adopt in response."-Gordon Livingston

514. "You're only given a little spark of madness. You mustn't lose it."-Robin Williams

515. "Does't thou love life? Then do not squander time, for that is the stuff that life is made of."-Benjamin Franklin

516. "A man's errors are his portals of discovery."-James Joyce

517. "Who finds a faithful friend, finds a treasure."-Jewish proverb

518. "Life is either a daring adventure or nothing."-Helen Keller

519. "As a culture, we seem to have trouble distinguishing science from pseudoscience, history from pseudohistory, and sense from nonsense."-Michael Shermer

520. "The clock of time is wound but once
And no man has the power
To tell you when his hands will stop
At late or early hour.
Now is the only time you own.
Live, love, toil with a will.

Place no faith in tomorrow
For the clock may then be still."-Durban

521. "The challenge of modernity is to live without illusions and without becoming disillusioned."-Antonio Gramsci

522. "Some cause happiness wherever they go; others, whenever they go."-Oscar Wilde

523. "Too many of us believe the world is to be discovered, rather than a product of our own construction and thus to be invented."-Ellen J Langer

524. "We are reformers in spring and summer, in autumn and winter we stand by the old; reformers in the morning, conservatives at night. Reform is affirmative, conservatism is negative; conservatism goes for comfort, reform for truth."-Ralph Waldo Emerson

525. "Every closed eye is not sleeping and every open eye is not seeing."-Bill Cosby

526. "Better keep yourself clean and bright; you are the window through which you must see the world."-George Bernard Shaw

527. "I am an optimist. It does not seem to be much use being anything else."-Winston Churchill

528. "Let no man pull you low enough to hate him."-Martin Luther King

529. "Search for knowledge from the cradle to the grave."-prophet Mohammed

530. "Whenever two people meet, there are really six people present. There is each man as he sees himself, each man as the other person sees him, and each man as he really is."-William James

531. "Well done is better than well said."-Benjamin Franklin

532. "If we want things to stay as they are, things will have to change."-Giuseppe Tomasi Di Lampedusa

533. "I expect to pass through life but once. If therefore, there be any kindness I can show, or any good thing I can do to any fellow being, let me do it now, and not defer or neglect it, as I shall not pass this way again."-William Penn

534. "To fear love is to fear life, and those who fear life are already three parts dead."- Bertrand Russell

535. "A goal without a plan is just a wish."-Antoine de Saint-Exupery

536. "Keep your face to the sunshine and you will not see the shadows."-Helen Keller

537. "Truly great friends are hard to find, difficult to leave, and impossible to forget."-G. Randolf

538. "Everything passes away - suffering, pain, blood, hunger, pestilence. The sword will pass away too, but the stars will still remain when the shadows of our presence and our deeds have vanished from the earth. There is no man who does not know that. Why, then, will we not turn our eyes towards the stars? Why?"-Mikhail Bulgakov

539. "When one door of happiness closes another opens; but often we look so long at the closed door that we do not see the one which has been opened for us."-Helen Keller

540. "Only those who risk going too far can possibly find out how far they can go."-T.S. Eliot

541. "Science goes out in search of greater truth (if it has to use the word truth at all) rather than the truth."-Christopher Potter

542. "Friendship doubles our joy and divides our grief."-Swedish proverb

543. "Success is getting what you want. Happiness is wanting what you get."-Dale Carnegie

544. "It's only those who do nothing who make no mistakes."-Joseph Conrad

545. "Life isn't about waiting for the storm to pass but learning to dance in the rain."-Anonymous

546. "Reading is to the mind what exercise is to the body."-Joseph Addison

547. "The hefty price for accepting information uncritically is that we go through life unaware that what we've accepted as impossible may in fact be quite possible."-Ellen J Langer

548. "Life is like riding a bicycle. To keep your balance you must keep moving."-Albert Einstein

549. "Describe the challenges by all means, but don't confuse analysis with action. The one must lead to the other if it is to be useful to people."-Michael Foot

550. "Time is what we want most, but what we use worst."-William Penn

551. "We know what we are, but know not what we may be."-William Shakespeare

552. "Common sense is the genius of humanity."-Johann Wolfgang von Goethe

553. "An exaggeration is a truth that has lost its temper."-Khalil Gibran

554. "The bad news is time flies. The good news is you're the pilot."-Michael Altshuler

555. "All I ask for in life is a soft bed and a library card. Everything else is extra."-Leon Malkin

556. "There is more to life than increasing its speed."-Mahatma Gandhi

557. "Diligence is the mother of good luck."-Benjamin Franklin

558. "Attitude is a little thing that makes a big difference."-Winston Churchill

559. "There is a wisdom in knowing when to resist, when to persist, and when to desist."-Jennifer Crokaert

560. "It is in the character of growth that we should learn from both pleasant and unpleasant experiences."-Nelson Mandela

561. "It is not true that people stop pursuing dreams because they grow old; they grow old because they stop pursuing dreams."-Gabriel Garcia Marquez

562. "Be like a tree; people throw stones at it but it throws down fruits at them."--Arabic

**563.** "No man is an island, entire of itself; every man is a piece of the continent, a part of the main." - John Donne

**564.** "I think there's just one kind of folks. Folks." -Harper Lee

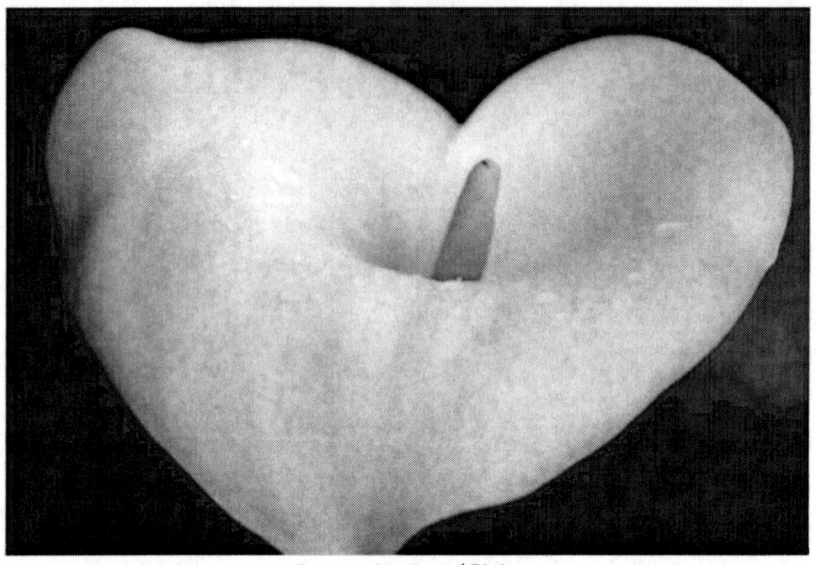

Cassandra Rae/flickr
http://www.flickr.com/photos/9100850@N04/4521706323/in/photolist

**565.** "The suffering of the people of any single country affects all of us no matter where we find ourselves."-Nelson Mandela

**566.** "I keep my friends as misers do their treasure because, of all things granted to us by wisdom, none is greater or better than friendship."-Pietro Aretino

**567.** "All truly great thoughts are conceived while walking."-Friedrich Nietzsche

**568.** "Keep calm and carry on."-British Government

**569.** "Life is too short and precious for us to pass through it without leaving a few footprints behind us."-Chiang Yee

**570.** "It's a little embarrassing that, after 45 years of research and study, the best advice I can give to people is to be a little kinder to each other."-Aldous Huxley

**571.** "The first hurdle is the people who will not accept the change that's already happened."-Joss Whedon

**572.** "Gifts make friends and friends make gifts."-Marshall Sahlins

**573.** "Nothing wondrous can come in this world unless it rests on the shoulders of kindness."-Barbara Kingsolver

**574.** "There is nothing in a caterpillar that tells you it is going to be a butterfly."-Buckminster Fuller

**575.** "Every experience in life, everything with which we have come in contact in life, is a chisel which has been cutting away at our life statue, moulding, modifying, shaping it. We are part of all we have met. Everything we have seen, heard, felt, or thought has had its hand in moulding us, shaping us."-Orison SwettMarden

**576.** "Always be kind, for everyone is fighting a hard battle."–Plato

577. "In times of change, learners will inherit the earth while the learned will find themselves beautifully equipped to deal with a world that no longer exists."-Eric Hoffer

578. "The work goes on, the cause endures, the hope still lives, and the dream shall never die."-Senator Edward Kennedy

579. "The best portion of a good man's life is his little, nameless, unremembered acts of kindness."-William Wordsworth

580. "Live as if you were to die tomorrow. Learn as if you were to live forever."-Mahatma Gandhi

581. "Nobody has the power to make you miserable - it's an inside job."-Adyashanti

582. "Never, never be afraid to do what's right, especially if the well-being of a person or animal is at stake. Society's punishments are small compared to the wounds we inflict on our soul when we look the other way."-Martin Luther King

583. "Do not judge your neighbor until you walk two moons in his moccasins."-Northern Cheyenne

584. "To be without some of the things you want is an indispensable part of happiness."-Bertrand Russell

585. "Don't judge each day by the harvest you reap, but by the seeds that you plant."-Robert Louis Stevenson

**586.** "Hope is not a feeling or a mood or a personality type. Hope is a choice."-Jim Wallis

**587.** "The greatest strength is gentleness."—Iroquois

**588.** "What is tolerance? It is the consequence of humanity. We are all formed of frailty and error; let us pardon reciprocally each other's folly - that is the first law of nature."-Francois-Marie Arouet

**589.** "Be at war with your vices, at peace with your neighbors, and let every new year find you a better man."-Benjamin Franklin

**590.** "Many persons have a wrong idea of what constitutes true happiness. It is not attained through self-gratification but through fidelity to a worthy purpose."-Helen Keller

**591.** "Do not dwell in the past, do not dream of the future, concentrate the mind on the present moment."—Buddha

**592.** "I brought children into this dark world because it needed the light that only a child can bring."-Liz Armbruster

**593.** "Keep me away from the wisdom which does not cry, the philosophy which does not laugh, and the greatness which does not bow before children."-Khalil Gibran

**594.** "We need to give each other the space to grow, to be ourselves, to exercise our diversity. We need to give each other space so that we may both give and receive such beautiful things as ideas, openness, dignity, joy, healing, and inclusion."-Max de Pree

595. "Fellowship is heaven, and lack of fellowship is hell; fellowship is life, and lack of fellowship is death; and the deeds that ye do upon the earth, it is for fellowship's sake that ye do them."-William Morris

596. "The things you really need are few and easy to come by; but the things you can imagine you need are infinite, and you will never be satisfied."–Epicurus

597. "Any fool can criticize, condemn and complain and most fools do."-Benjamin Franklin

598. "There is one way of attaining what we may term, if not utter, at least mortal happiness; it is by a sincere and unrelaxing activity for the happiness of others."-Edward Bulwer-Lytton

599. "Those who have one foot in the canoe and one foot in the boat are going to fall in the river."–Tuscarora

600. "Act as if what you do makes a difference. It does."-William James

601. "You give but little when you give of your possessions. It is when you give of yourself that you truly give."-Khalil Gibran

momo/flickr
http://www.flickr.com/photos/9751325@N02/7277580944/in/photolist

602. "An investment in knowledge pays the best interest."-Benjamin Franklin

603. "Since there is nothing so well worth having as friends, never lose a chance to make them."-Guicciardini

604. "Just because you're breathing doesn't mean you're alive."–Edge

605. "A goal without a plan is a dream and dreams fade when we awake."-Jannie Williams

606. "The older you get, the more you realize that kindness is synonymous with happiness."-Lionel Barrymore

**607.** "If you want others to be happy, practice compassion. If you want to be happy, practice compassion."- Dalai Lama

**608.** "Live more. Give more. Forgive more."-TrudieStyler

**609.** "Life is about not knowing, having to change, taking the moment and making the best of it, without knowing what's going to happen next. Delicious ambiguity."-Gilda Radner

**610.** "Remember a real decision is measured by the fact that you've taken new action; if there's no action, you haven't truly decided."-Anthony Robbins

**611.** "Sandwich every bit of criticism between two thick layers of praise."-Mary Kay Ash

**612.** "Absence sharpens love, presence strengthens it."-Benjamin Franklin

**613.** "Each day comes bearing its own gifts. Untie the ribbons."-Ruth Ann Schabacker

**614.** "The fool wonders; the wise man asks."-Benjamin Disraeli

**615.** "To be happy in this world, especially when youth is past, it is necessary to feel oneself not merely an isolated individual whose day will soon be over, but part of the stream of life flowing on from the first germ to the remote and unknown future."-Bertrand Russell

**616.** "Wisdom begins in wonder."- Socrates

**617.** "We tend to forget that happiness doesn't come as a result of getting something we don't have, but rather of recognizing and appreciating what we do have."-Frederich Koenig

**618.** "The most important thing in communication is to hear what isn't being said."-Peter Drucker

**619.** "The earth is not given to us by our parents; it is lent to us by our children."-Kenyan proverb

**620.** "The person who has lived the most is not the one with the most years but the one with the richest experiences."-Jean Jacques Rousseau

**621.** "A wonderful fact to reflect upon, that every human creature is constituted to be that profound secret and mystery to every other."-Charles Dickens

**622.** "Learn all you can from the mistakes of others. You won't have time to make them all yourself."-Alfred Sheinwold

**623.** "Life may not be the party we hoped for, but while we are here we might as well dance."-Anonymous

**624.** "Do not fear to open the doors that lie between what is known and what is unknown."-Wayne Dyer

625. "The smallest act of kindness is worth more than the grandest intention."- Oscar Wilde

626. "He is richest who is content with the least, for contentment is the wealth of nature."-Socrates

627. "What we have done for ourselves alone dies with us."- Albert Pike

628. "Everybody likes a compliment."-Abraham Lincoln

629. "It isn't our position, but our disposition, that makes us happy."- Anonymous

630. "Anything worth doing is going to be difficult."-Unknown

631. "Kindness is a language which the deaf can hear and the blind can see."- Mark Twain

632. "Doubting everything or believing everything are two equally convenient solutions, both of which save us from thinking."-Henri Poincaré

633. "Two things you should never be angry at: what you can help and what you cannot help."-Thomas Fuller

634. "It is preoccupation with possessions, more than anything else, that prevents us from living freely and nobly."-Bertrand Russell

**635.** "You can't think your way into a new way of living; you have to live your way into a new way of thinking."- Wayne Dyer

**636.** "The test of our progress is not whether we add more to the abundance of those who have much, it is whether we provide enough for those who have too little."- Eleanor Roosevelt

**637.** "There is only one way to happiness and that is to cease worrying about things which are beyond the power of our will."- Epictetus

**638.** "I wanted a perfect ending. Now I've learned, the hard way, that some poems don't rhyme, and some stories don't have a clear beginning, middle and end. Life is about not knowing, having to change, taking the moment and making the best of it, without knowing what's going to happen next. Delicious ambiguity."- Gilda Radner

**639.** "Happiness is the meaning and purpose of life, the whole aim and end of human existence."-Aristotle

**640.** "How wonderful it is that nobody need wait a single moment before starting to improve the world."-Anne Frank

**641.** "Poverty is the worst form of violence."-Mahatma Gandhi

**642.** "Be glad of life because it gives you the chance to love and to work and to play and to look up at the stars."- Henry van Dyke

643. "The value systems of those with access to power and of those far removed from such access cannot be the same. The viewpoint of the privileged is unlike that of the underprivileged.Aung San SuuKyi

644. "All who would win joy must share it; happiness was born a twin."- Lord Byron

645. "Annual income twenty pounds, annual expenditure nineteen, nineteen, six, result happiness. Annual income twenty pounds, annual expenditure twenty pounds, nought, and six, result misery."-MrMicawber

646. "Liberty produces wealth, and wealth destroys liberty."- Henry Demarest Lloyd

647. "Be kind, for everyone you meet is fighting a hard battle."-Philo

648. "Everything will be alright in the end. If it is not alright, then it is not the end."- Exotic Marigold

649. "The bridges you cross before you come to them are over rivers that aren't there."-Gene Brown

650. "A kind word can warm three winter months."- Japanese proverb

**651.** "An individual has not started living until he can rise above the narrow confines of his individualistic concerns to the broader concerns of all humanity."- Martin Luther King

**652.** "A kind word is like a Springday."- Russian proverb

**653.** "Without inspiration the best powers of the mind remain dormant. There is a fuel in us which needs to be ignited with sparks."-Johann Gottfried von Herder

**654.** "Approximately half of the world's one hundred largest economic entities are now corporations"-Rebecca MacKinnon

**655.** "If your dreams do not scare you, they are not big enough."- Ellen Johnson Sirleaf

**656.** "A human being is a part of the whole, called by us 'Universe,' a part limited in time and space. He experiences himself, his thoughts, and feelings as something separated from the rest, a kind of optical delusion of his consciousness. This delusion is a kind of prison for us, restricting us to our personal desires and to affection for a few persons nearest to us. Our task must be to free ourselves from this prison by widening our circle of compassion to embrace all living creatures and the whole of nature in its beauty. Nobody is able to achieve this completely, but the striving for such achievement is in itself a part of the liberation and a foundation for inner security."-Albert Einstein

**657.** "Wise sayings often fall on barren ground, but a kind word is never thrown away."-Arthur Helps

658. "The past is never dead. It's not even past."- William Faulkner

659. "There's nothing simpler than looking at the goodness in other people. The difficult part is to tell them what you see."-John Mooney

660. "Our doubts are traitors, and make us lose the good we oft might win by fearing to attempt."-William Shakespeare

661. "Always dream and shoot higher than you know you can do. Don't bother just to be better than your contemporaries or predecessors. Try to be better than yourself."-William Faulkner

662. "Our lives begin to end the day we become silent about things that matter."-Martin Luther King

663. "Man is a knot, a web, a mesh into which relationships are tied. Only those relationships matter."-Antoine de Saint-Exupery

664. "One who knows how to show and to accept kindness will be a friend better than any possession."- Sophocles

665. "You will find yourself refreshed by the presence of cheerful people. Why not make earnest effort to confer that pleasure on others?"-Lydia M Child

666. "There is no exercise better for the heart than reaching down and lifting people up."-John Albert Holmes

667. "Since there is nothing so well worth having as friends, never lose a chance to make them."-Francesco Guicciardini

668. "To laugh often and love much; to win the respect of intelligent persons and the affection of children; to earn the approbation of honest citizens and endure the betrayal of false friends; to appreciate beauty; to find the best in others; to give of one's self; to leave the world a bit better, whether by a healthy child, a garden patch or a redeemed social condition; to have played and laughed with enthusiasm and sung with exultation; to know even one life has breathed easier because you have lived - this is to have succeeded."-Ralph Waldo Emerson

669. "Know that joy is rarer, more difficult, and more beautiful than sadness. Once you make this all-important discovery, you must embrace joy as a moral obligation."-André Gide

670. "Happiness is not a destination; it is a way of life."–Porvoo

671. "Thoughts lead on to purposes; purposes go forth in action; actions form habits; habits decide character; and character fixes our destiny."- Tyron Edwards

672. "Though we all have the fear and the seeds of anger within us, we must learn not to water those seeds and instead nourish our positive qualities – those of compassion, understanding, and loving kindness."-ThichNhatHanh

673. "Look up at the stars and not down at your feet. Try to make sense of what you see and wonder about what makes the universe exist. Be curious."-Professor Stephen Hawking

Just a Prairie Boy/flickr
http://www.flickr.com/photos/89679291@N00/4840178658/in/photolist

674. "The aim of education should be to teach us rather how to think, than what to think - rather to improve our minds, so as to enable us to think for ourselves, than to load the memory with the thoughts of other men."- John Dewey

675. "Abundance is not something we acquire. It is something we tune into." - Wayne Dyer

676. "I have observed that those who so violently condemn wealth are precisely those who do not have it and see no way of personally gaining it. They take the fear of failure and translate it into the love of poverty. If I say that I do not want wealth,

then I do not have to deal with reality. I do not have to face that awful truth that perhaps I must change." - Thomas D. Willhite

677. "Not what we have but what we enjoy, constitutes our abundance." - John Petit-Senn

678. "The real issue is value, not price." - Robert T. Lindgren

679. "Successful people make money. It's not that people who make money become successful, but that successful people attract money. They bring success to what they do." - Wayne Dyer

680. "Prosperity depends more on wanting what you have than having what you want." - Geoffrey F. Abert

681. "The man is richest whose pleasures are cheapest." - Henry David Thoreau

682. "An investment in knowledge always pays the best interest." - Benjamin Franklin

683. "It is only when people shake off the baggage of financial misinformation they have acquired from their parents, teachers, friends and past financial disasters that they are able to advance themselves financially." - Todd Dean

684. "A company's character is known by the people it keeps." - John Ruskin

685. "Never continue in a job you don't enjoy. If you're happy in what you're doing, you'll like yourself, you'll have inner peace. And if you have that, along with physical health, you will have had more success than you could possibly have imagined." - Johnny Carson

686. "The master in the art of living makes little distinction between his work and his play, his labor and his leisure, his mind and his body, his information and his recreation, his love and his religion. He hardly knows which is which. He simply pursues his vision of excellence at whatever he does, leaving others to decide whether he is working or playing. To him he's always doing both." - James A. Michener

687. "The main thing is to keep the main thing the main thing." - Steven Covey

688. "When a Company compromises its principles one time, the next compromise is right around the corner." - Zig Ziglar

689. "I want to be thoroughly used up when I die, for the harder I work the more I live. I rejoice in life for its own sake." - George Bernard Shaw

690. "The true way to render ourselves happy is to love our work and find in it our pleasure." - Francoise de Motteville

691. "There's just a slight difference in the spelling between Hard working and Hardly working but once either is followed can lead to results with greatest variations." - Ritika Chopra

692. "Opportunity is missed by most because it is dressed in overalls and looks like work." - Thomas Edison

693. "Do not hire a man who does your work for money, but him who does it for love of it." - Henry David Thoreau

694. "Find a job you like and you add five days to every week." - H. Jackson Brown, Jr.

695. "I can't imagine anything more worthwhile than doing what I most love. And they pay me for it." - Edgar Winter

696. "The harder I work, the luckier I get." - Samuel Goldwyn

697. "The only place success comes before work is in the dictionary." - Vince Lombardi

698. "There is no substitute for hard work." - Thomas A. Edison

699. "Laziness may appear attractive, but work gives satisfaction." - nne Frank

700. "Nothing will work unless you do." - Maya Angelou

701. "I don't even think you know how great you really are. I believe in you." -Dick Vermeil

702. "Believe deep down in your heart that you're destined to do great things." -Joe Paterno

703. "There's a reason why today is called the present. It is a gift you have been given to live another day and enjoy everything around you because no one is guaranteed a tomorrow." -Jeff Laforteza

704. "I don't believe make-up and the right hairstyle alone can make a woman beautiful. The most radiant woman in the room is the one full of life and experience." – Unknown

705. "Listening can heal wounds." -Sean Covey

706. "When we allow ourselves to become vulnerable, to take chances, and to risk our pride, that is when we find our own glory." -Richard Corman

707. "Keep your dreams alive. Understand to achieve anything requires faith and belief in yourself, vision, hard work,

determination, and dedication. Remember all things are possible for those who believe." -Gail Devers

708.  "The moment of enlightenment is when a person's dreams of possibilities become images of probabilities." -Vic Braden

709.  "Dreams come a size too big so that we can grow into them." - Josie Bisset

710.  "For everyone of us that succeeds, it's because there's somebody there to show you the way out. The light doesn't always necessarily have to be in your family; for me it was teachers and school." -Oprah Winfrey

711.  "Lying in bed just before going to sleep is the worst time for organized thinking; it is the best time for free thinking. Ideas drift like clouds in an undecided breeze, taking first this direction and then that." -E.L. Konigsburg

712.  "All kids need is a little help, a little hope and somebody who believes in them." -Earvin "Magic" Johnson

713.  "The young do not know enough to be prudent, and therefore they attempt the impossible--and achieve it." -Pearl Buck

714.  "We should all do what, in the long run, gives us joy, even if it is only picking grapes or sorting the laundry." -E.B. White

715.  "Balance isn't about moderation, it's about admitting what's really important to you. Someone might reach 16 years of age with a terrible thirst to play music, or soccer, or earn money, and their idea of balance is to spend 90% of their time doing just that." – Unknown

716.  "The strongest oak tree of the forest is not the one that is protected from the storm and hidden from the sun. It's the one

that stands in the open where it is compelled to struggle for its existence against the winds and rains and the scorching sun." - Napoleon Hill

717. "Angels do find us in our hour of need." -Amy Huffman

718. "A truly great person is the one who gives you a chance." - Paul Duffy

719. "For those who are willing to make an effort, great miracles and wonderful treasures are in store." –

720. "A Tale of Three Wishes" - by Isaac Bashevis Singer

721. "We weep over the graves of infants and the little ones taken from us by death; but an early grave may be the shortest way to heaven." -Tryon Edwards

722. "A bird does not fear falling for it has never fallen before. So we must act as the bird and block out our fears. Then we will be able to soar higher than we ever imagined." -Kevin Wassie

723. "There is great significance and importance in all our day-to-day actions in both words and deeds." -Jennifer Leigh Youngs

724. "We are all intertwined, each desperately loved and needed by others." -S.O.L.O.S.

725. "True courage is to stand against evil, even when we stand alone." -Richard Edgely

726. "Do not regret growing old. It is a privilege denied to many." – Unknown

727. "Memory is a way of holding onto the things you love, the things you are, the things you never want to lose." -Keven Arnold (Fred Savage),The Wonder Years

728. "Honesty is a principle. Service is a principle. Love is a principle. Hard work is a principle. Respect, gratitude, moderation, fairness, integrity, loyalty, and responsibility are principles. There are dozens and dozens more. They are not hard to identify. Just as a compass always points to true north, your heart will recognize true principles." -Sean Covey

729. "With the new day comes new strength and new thoughts." -Eleanor Roosevelt

730. "A child is like a piece of paper on which every passerby leaves a mark." -Chinese proverb

731. "No one's death comes to pass without making some impression, and those close to the deceased inherit part of the liberated soul and become richer in their humanness." -Hermann Broch

732. "I believe there are angels among us, sent down to us from somewhere up above. They come to you and me in our darkest hours, to show us how to live, to teach us how to give, to guide us with a light of love." -Alabama, "Angels Among Us"

733. "All the world is full of suffering. It is also full of overcoming." -Helen Keller

734. "We are troubled, but we have hope and tremendous promise." -Sara Shandler

735. "The greatest possession we have costs nothing; it's known as love." -Brian Jett

**736.** "Good Enough is the enemy of excellence." – Unknown

**737.** "Whatever you can do or dream you can, begin it. Boldness has genius, power and magic in it." – Johann Wolfgang von Goethe

**738.** "Achievement seems to be connected with action. Successful men and women keep moving. They make mistakes, but they don't quit." – Conrad Hilton

**739.** "Confidence doesn't come out of nowhere. It's a result of something... hours and days and weeks and years of constant work and dedication." - Roger Staubach

**740.** "Develop the winning edge; small differences in your performance can lead to large differences in your results." - Brian Tracy

**741.** "Just as some plants bear fruit only if they don't shoot up too high, so in practical arts the leaves and flowers of theory must be pruned and the plant kept close to its proper soil - experience." - Carl von Clausewitz

**742.** "It's not whether you get knocked down, It's whether you get up again." - Vince Lombardi

**743.** "The only time success comes before work is in the dictionary." - Unknown

**744.** "Since most of us spend our lives doing ordinary tasks, the most important thing is to carry them out extraordinarily well." - Henry David Thoreau

**745.** "Excellence is not a destination; it is a continuous journey that never ends." – Brian Tracy

746. "Optimism means expecting the best, but confidence means knowing how to handle the worst. Never make a move if you are merely optimistic." – The Zurich Axioms

747. "To win without risk is to triumph without glory." – Pierre Corneille

748. "Carry the battle to them. Don't let them bring it to you. Put them on the defensive. And don't ever apologize for anything." – Harry S. Truman

749. "A pessimist sees the difficulty in every opportunity; an optimist sees the opportunity in every difficulty." - Sir Winston Churchill

750. "It is in the compelling zest of high adventure and of victory, and in creative action, that man finds his supreme joys." - Antoine de Saint-Exupery

751. "Life is a series of experiences, each one of which makes us bigger.... For the world was built to develop character, and we must learn that the setbacks and griefs we endure help us in our marching onward." – Henry Ford

752. "The longer I live, the more I am certain that the great difference between the great and insignificant is energy – invincible determination – a purpose once fixed and then death or victory." – Sir Thomas Fowell Buxton

753. "Only through focus can you do world-class things, no matter how capable you are." - Bill Gates

754. "Learning is not attained by chance. It must be sought for with ardor and attended to with diligence." Abigail Adams

755. "The credit belongs to the man who is actually in the arena; whose face is marred by dust and sweat and blood; who strives valiantly; who errs and comes short again and again; who knows the great enthusiasms, the great devotions, and spends himself in a worthy cause; who at the best knows in the end the triumph of high achievement; and who at the worst, if he fails, at least fails while daring greatly." - Theodore Roosevelt

756. "The fundamental demand for a first-rate Go player, or any other athlete, is to strive for excellence in order to obtain the crown of performance. In competition it is usually imperative for the competitor to maintain a purely contestative state of mind, with his mind undisturbed and concentrated on the fight. A player must aim high, keep improving and perfecting his skills; in a word, he must surpass his limits. This is also required of the promising younger generation of crack players who have made remarkable achievements in order to meet the challenge from his opponent with open and magnanimous mind. Life is a continuous process of discovering one's mistakes, errors, weaknesses, a process of transcendence in which on progresses toward the ultimate goal. This applies also to the issue of life or death, which must be tackled with a sustained mentality of transcendence. This is an optimistic attitude." - Chen Zude

757. "Everything depends upon execution; having just a vision is no solution." – Stephen Sondheim

758. "The definition of insanity is doing the same thing over and over again and expecting a different result." - Albert Einstein

759. "Being defeated is often only a temporary condition. Giving up is what makes it permanent." - Marilyn vos Savant

760. "At first our dreams seem impossible, then they seem improbable, but when we summon the will, they become inevitable." – Christopher Reeve

761. "Ultimately, man should not ask what the meaning of his life is, but rather must recognize that it is he who is asked. In a word, each man is questioned by life; and he can only answer to life by answering for his own life; to life he can only respond by being responsible." - Victor Frankl

762. "Impossible. The word itself tells: I m possible." - Unknown

763. "Determine that the thing can and shall be done, and then we shall find the way." - Abraham Lincoln

764. "I can't imagine a person becoming a success who doesn't give this game of life everything he's got." – Walter Cronkite

765. "The ability to discipline yourself to delay gratification in the short term in order to enjoy greater rewards in the long term is the indispensable prerequisite for success." - Brian Tracy

766. "Rowing harder doesn't help if the boat is headed in the wrong direction." - Kenichi Ohmae

767. "The will to win is important, but the will to prepare is vital." - Joe Paterno

768. "Everyone who got where he is had to begin where he was." - Robert Louis Stevenson

769. "If you aren't going to go all the way, why go at all? " - Joe Namath

770. "The path to success is to take massive, determined action." - Anthony Robbins

771. "Tell me and I'll forget. Show me and I may remember. Involve me and I'll understand." - Unknown

772. "The reading of all good books is indeed like a conversation with the noblest men of past centuries who were the authors of them, nay a carefully studied conversation, in which they reveal to us none but the best of their thoughts." – Rene Descartes

773. "Far better it is to dare mighty things, to win glorious triumphs, even though checkered by failure...than to rank with those poor spirits who neither enjoy much nor suffer much, because they live in a gray twilight that knows not victory nor defeat." - Theodore Roosevelt

774. "I used to say, 'I sure hope things will change.' Then I learned that the only way things are going to change for me is when I change." – Jim Rohn

775. "When you cannot make up your mind which of the two evenly balanced courses of action you should take, choose the bolder." - W. J. Slim

776. "Courage is the ladder on which all the other virtues mount." - Clare Booth Luce

777. "If a man has talent and cannot use it, he has failed. If he has talent and only uses half of it, he has partly failed. If he has talent and learns somehow to use the whole of it, he has gloriously succeeded and won satisfaction and a triumph few men ever know." - Thomas Wolfe

778. "I know the price of success: dedication, hard work and an unremitting devotion to the things you want to see happen." - Frank Lloyd Wright

779. "We cannot build our own future without helping others to build theirs." -Bill Clinton

780. "Sometimes when people are under stress, they hate to think, and it's the time when they most need to think." -Bill Clinton

781. "We don't know a millionth of one percent about anything." -Thomas Edison

782. "There is no substitute for hard work."-Thomas Edison

783. "Opportunity is missed by most people because it is dressed in overalls and looks like work."-Thomas Edison

784. "The first requisite for success is the ability to apply your physical and mental energies to one problem incessantly without growing weary." -Thomas Edison

785. "Genius is one per cent inspiration, ninety-nine per cent perspiration." -Thomas Edison

786. "I am not discouraged, because every wrong attempt discarded is another step forward." -Thomas Edison

787. "There is always a better way." -Thomas Edison

788. "Anything you really want, you can attain, if you really go after it."-Wayne Dyer

789. "Be miserable. Or motivate yourself. Whatever has to be done, it's always your choice."-Wayne Dyer

790. "Conflict cannot survive without your participation." -Wayne Dyer

791. "Deficiency motivation doesn't work. It will lead to a life-long pursuit of try to fix me. Learn to appreciate what you have and where and who you are." -Wayne Dyer

792. "Success is not the measure of a man but a triumph over those who choose to hold him back."-Bill Clinton

793. "We should, all of us, be filled with gratitude and humility for our present progress and prosperity. We should be filled with awe and joy at what lies over the horizon. And we should be filled with absolute determination to make the most of it."-Bill Clinton

794. "By lifting the weakest, poorest among us, we lift the rest of us as well."-Bill Clinton

795. "Keep your eyes on the prize and don't turn back."-Bill Clinton

796. "Pessimism is an excuse for not trying and a guarantee to a personal failure."-Bill Clinton

797. "Strength and wisdom are not opposing values."-Bill Clinton

798. "Doing what you love is the cornerstone of having abundance in your life." -Wayne Dyer

799. "Everything in the universe has a purpose. Indeed, the invisible intelligence that flows through everything in a purposeful fashion is also flowing through you." -Wayne Dyer

800. "Everything is perfect in the universe - even your desire to improve it." -Wayne Dyer

801. "Everything you are against weakens you. Everything you are for empowers you." -Wayne Dyer

802. "Go for it now. The future is promised to no one."-Wayne Dyer

803. "How people treat you is their karma; how you react is yours." -Wayne Dyer

804. "I cannot always control what goes on outside. But I can always control what goes on inside." -Wayne Dyer

805. "If you change the way you look at things, the things you look at change." -Wayne Dyer

806. "It is impossible for you to be angry and laugh at the same time. Anger and laughter are mutually exclusive and you have the poser to choose either."
-Wayne Dyer

807. "It makes no sense to worry about things you have no control over because there's nothing you can do about them, and why worry about things you do control? The activity of worrying keeps you immobilized." -Wayne Dyer

808. "It's never crowded along the extra mile."-Wayne Dyer

809. "Our intention creates our reality." -Wayne Dyer

810. "Self-worth comes from one thing - thinking that you are worthy."
-Wayne Dyer

811. "Stop acting as if life is a rehearsal. Live this day as if it were your last. The past is over and gone. The future is not guaranteed." -Wayne Dyer

812. "Successful people make money. It's not that people who make money become successful, but that successful people attract money. They bring success to what they do." -Wayne Dyer

813. "The components of anxiety, stress, fear, and anger do not exist independently of you in the world. They simply do not exist in the physical world, even though we talk about them as if they do." - Wayne Dyer

814. "There is no scarcity of opportunity to make a living at what you love; there's only scarcity of resolve to make it happen." - Wayne Dyer

815. "There is no way to prosperity, prosperity is the way." - Wayne Dyer

816. "What comes out of you when you are squeezed is what is inside of you."
-Wayne Dyer

817. "What we think determines what happens to us, so if we want to change our lives, we need to stretch our minds." -Wayne Dyer

818. "You cannot always control what goes on outside. But you can always control what goes on inside."-Wayne Dyer

819. "You leave old habits behind by starting out with the thought, 'I release the need for this in my life."-Wayne Dyer

820. "Effective leadership is putting first things first. Effective management is discipline, carrying it out."-Stephen Covey

821. "Every human has four endowments- self awareness, conscience, independent will and creative imagination. These give us the ultimate human freedom... The power to choose, to respond, to change."-Stephen Covey

822. "In the last analysis, what we are communicates far more eloquently than anything we say or do." -Stephen Covey

823. "Live out of your imagination, not your history." -Stephen Covey

824. "Management is efficiency in climbing the ladder of success; leadership determines whether the ladder is leaning against the right wall."-Stephen Covey

825. "Our character is basically a composite of our habits. Because they are consistent, often unconscious patterns, they constantly, daily, express our character." -Stephen Covey

826. "The key is not to prioritize what's on your schedule, but to schedule your priorities."-Stephen Covey

827. "The main thing is to keep the main thing the main thing."-Stephen Covey

828. "There are three constants in life... change, choice and principles." -Stephen Covey

829. "We are not animals. We are not a product of what has happened to us in our past. We have the power of choice." -Stephen Covey

830. "We are the creative force of our life, and through our own decisions rather than our conditions, if we carefully learn to do certain things, we can accomplish those goals." -Stephen Covey

831. "Mental toughness is to physical as four is to one."-Bobby Knight

832. "The will to win means nothing without the will to prepare."-Juma Ikangaa

833. "A winner never stops trying." -Tom Landry

834. "I don't believe in team motivation. I believe in getting a team prepared so it knows it will have the necessary confidence when it steps on a field and be prepared to play a good game."-Tom Landry

835. "I've learned that something constructive comes from every defeat."-Tom Landry

836. "If you are prepared, you will be confident, and will do the job."-Tom Landry

837. "Setting a goal is not the main thing. It is deciding how you will go about achieving it and staying with that plan."-Tom Landry

838. "The secret to winning is constant, consistent management." -Tom Landry

839. "Today, you have 100% of your life left." -Tom Landry

**840.** "When you want to win a game, you have to teach. When you lose a game, you have to learn."-Tom Landry

**841.**

"Always keep an open mind and a compassionate heart." -Phil Jackson

**842.** "Wisdom is always an overmatch for strength." -Phil Jackson

**843.** "People who live in the past generally are afraid to compete in the present. I've got my faults, but living in the past is not one of them. There's no future in it."
-Sparky Anderson

**844.** "Success is the person who year after year reaches the highest limits in his field."
-Sparky Anderson

**845.** "A winner is someone who recognizes his God-given talents, works his tail off to develop them into skills, and uses these skills to accomplish his goals." -Larry Bird

**846.** "I don't know if I practiced more than anybody, but I sure practiced enough. I still wonder if somebody - somewhere - was practicing more than me." -Larry Bird

**847.** "I've got a theory that if you give 100 percent all of the time, somehow things will work out in the end."-Larry Bird

**848.** "It doesn't matter who scores the points, it's who can get the ball to the scorer."
-Larry Bird

849. "Leadership is diving for a loose ball, getting the crowd involved, getting other players involved. It's being able to take it as well as dish it out. That's the only way you're going to get respect from the players." -Larry Bird

850. "Leadership is getting players to believe in you. If you tell a teammate you're ready to play as tough as you're able to, you'd better go out there and do it. Players will see right through a phony. And they can tell when you're not giving it all you've got."-Larry Bird

851. "Once you are labeled 'the best' you want to stay up there, and you can't do it by loafing around." -Larry Bird

852. "Push yourself again and again. Don't give an inch until the final buzzer sounds."
-Larry Bird

853. "Before you can win, you have to believe you are worthy."-Mike Ditka

854. "I really believe the only way to stay healthy is to eat properly, get your rest and exercise. If you don't exercise and do the other two, I still don't think it's going to help you that much." -Mike Ditka

855. "If you are determined enough and willing to pay the price, you can get it done."
-Mike Ditka

856. "Success isn't measured by money or power or social rank. Success is measured by your discipline and inner peace." -Mike Ditka

857. "Success isn't permanent and failure isn't fatal." -Mike Ditka

858. "The ones who want to achieve and win championships motivate themselves."
-Mike Ditka

859. "What you feel spiritually. I think a lot of that has to do with it. If you have no spiritual life, chances are everything is going to aggravate you, you're going to fly off the handle at everything and that's what I did in the past. I've kind of got that under control now." -Mike Ditka

860. "If you don't try — then there is NO experience."— Nicholas Marchan

861. "Sometimes in life you have to let things just roll off of you ... lest they make an ugly stain." — Author Unknown

862. "What this power is I cannot say; all I know is that it exists and it becomes available only when a man is in that state of mind in which he knows exactly what he wants and is fully determined not to quit until he finds it." — Alexander Graham Bell

863. "A ship in port is safe, but that's not what ships are built for." — Rear Admiral Grace Murray Hopper

864. "Whatever you do may seem insignificant to you, but it is most important that you do it." — Gandhi

865. "A woman is like a tea bag. She only knows her strength when put in hot water." — Nancy Reagan

866. "I find the great thing in this world is not so much where we stand, as in what direction we are moving; we must sail sometimes with the wind and sometimes against it ... but we must sail, and not drift, nor lie at anchor." — Oliver Wendell Holmes

867. "One of the secrets of life is to make stepping stones out of stumbling blocks." — Jack Penn

868. "Courage is not the absence of fear, but rather the judgment that something else is more important than fear." — Ambrose Redmoon

869. "When there is no wind ... ROW!" —Latin Proverb

870. "One of the best ways to get through difficulties is to simply persevere day by day. Huge projects don't seem as daunting when we focus on one element ... completing that before we tackle the next phase. As Napoleon Hill said, "Most great people have attained their greatest success just one step beyond their greatest failure." —Chelle Thompson

871. "One day, in retrospect, the years of struggle will strike you as the most beautiful." — Sigmund Freud

872. "Providence creates an unfolding situation that is exactly what the person needs, although not always what he may think he

wants or desires. This is called luck by those who are unaware of the workings of higher Worlds. Providence also creates very difficult circumstances to reveal or dissolve a fixed situation ... This is called bad luck or later, A Blessing in Disguise." — Warren Kenton

873. "We rest here while we can, but we hear the ocean calling in our dreams, And we know by the morning, the wind will fill our sails to test the seams. The calm is on the water and part of us would linger by the shore. For ships are safe in harbor, but that's not what ships are for." —Tom Kimmel & Michael Lille

874. "I never failed once. It just happened to be a 2000-step process." — Thomas Edison

875. "By and large, mothers and housewives are the only workers who do not have regular time off. They are the great vacationless class."— Anne Morrow Lindbergh

876. "Discovery consists of seeing what everybody has seen, and thinking what nobody has thought." — Albert Szent-Gyorgi

877. "The only way to discover the limits of the possible is to go beyond them into the impossible." —Arthur C. Clarke

878. "Challenges often make us realize that we have more courage than we think and that one person CAN make a difference in the world ... even if it's the world of one other person." — Chelle Thompson, Editor of Inspiration Line

879. "There have been so many times in my life when things that looked like disasters were really incredible GIFTS that served as pivotal turning points. I am truly thankful for persevering through all of my 'mistakes." —Chelle Thompson

880. "A keen sense of humor helps us to overlook the unbecoming, understand the unconventional, tolerate the unpleasant, overcome the unexpected, and outlast the unbearable." — Billy Graham

881. "The universe will reward you for taking risks on its behalf." — Shakti Gawain

882. "I am still learning — how to take joy in all the people I am, how to use all my selves in the service of what I believe, how to accept when I fail and rejoice when I succeed." — Audre Lorde, African-American Author

883. "Adversity introduces a man to himself." —Seneca, Roman Statesman and Philosopher

884. "Life's challenges are not supposed to paralyze you, they're supposed to help you discover who you are. " — Bernice Johnson Reagon

885. "Each choice we make causes a ripple effect in our lives. When things happen to us, it is the reaction we choose that can create the difference between the sorrows of our past and the joy in our future." —Chelle Thompson, Editor of Inspiration Line

886. "Nothing in this world can take the place of persistence. Talent will not; nothing is more common than unsuccessful people with talent. Genius will not; unrewarded genius is almost a proverb. Education will not; the world is full of educated derelicts. Persistence and determination alone are omnipotent. The slogan 'press on' has solved and always will solve the problems of the human race." — Calvin Coolidge

887. "As long as we are persistent in our pursuit of our deepest destiny, we will continue to grow. We cannot choose the day or time when we will fully bloom. It happens in its own time." — Denis Waitley

888. "If you have made mistakes, even serious ones, there is always another chance for you. What we call failure is not the falling down, but the staying down." — Mary Pickford

889. "The way to succeed is never quit. That's it. But really be humble about it." — Alex Haley

890. "Consider the postage stamp: its usefulness consists in the ability to stick to one thing until it gets there." — Josh Billings

891. "The difference between perseverance and obstinacy is that one comes from a strong will, and the other from a strong won't." — Henry Ward Beecher

892. "Great works are performed not by strength but by perseverance." — Samuel Johnson

893. "The greatest results in life are usually attained by simple means and the exercise of ordinary qualities. These may for the most part be summed up in these two — common sense and perseverance." — Owen Feltham

894. If I had to select one quality, one personal characteristic that I regard as being most highly correlated with success, whatever the field, I would pick the trait of persistence. Determination. The will to endure to the end, to get knocked down seventy times and get up off the floor saying, "Here comes number seventy-one!" — Richard M. Devos

895. "If you only knock long enough and loud enough at the gate, you are sure to wake up somebody." — Henry Wadsworth Longfellow

896. "In the confrontation between the stream and the rock, the stream always wins — not through strength but by perseverance." — H. Jackson Brown

897. "It's the constant and determined effort that breaks down all resistance, sweeps away all obstacles." — Claude M. Bristol

898. "Never measure the height of a mountain until you reach the top. Then you will see how low it was." — Dag Hammerskjold

899. "On the mountains of truth you can never climb in vain: either you will reach a point higher up today, or you will be training your powers so that you will be able to climb higher tomorrow." — Friedrich Nietzsche

900. "Some men give up their designs when they have almost reached the goal; While others, on the contrary, obtain a victory by exerting, at the last moment, more vigorous efforts than ever before." — Herodotus

901. "Success is not final, failure is not fatal: it is the courage to continue that counts."
— Sir Winston Churchill

902. "Success seems to be connected with action. Successful men keep moving. They make mistakes, but they don't quit." — Conrad Hilton

903. Tenacity is a pretty fair substitute for bravery, and the best form of tenacity I know is expressed in a Danish fur trapper's principle" "The next mile is the only one a person really has to make." — Eric Sevareid

904. "There is no chance, no destiny, no fate, that can circumvent or hinder or control the firm resolve of a determined soul." — Ella Wheeler Wilcox

905. "When you get into a tight place and everything goes against you, till it seems as though you could not hang on a minute longer, never give up then, for that is just the place and time that the tide will turn." — Harriet Beecher Stowe

906. "Above all, challenge yourself. You may well surprise yourself at what strengths you have, what you can accomplish." — Cecile M. Springer

**907.** "The big challenge is to become all that you have the possibility of becoming. You cannot believe what it does to the human spirit to maximize your human potential and stretch yourself to the limit." — Jim Rohn

**908.** "Challenge is the core and the mainspring of all human activity. If there's an ocean, we cross it; if there's a disease, we cure it; if there's a wrong, we right it; if there's a record, we break it; and finally, if there's a mountain, we climb it."
— James Ramesy Ullman

**909.** "The challenges of change are always hard. It is important that we begin to unpack those challenges that confront this nation and realize that we each have a role that requires us to change and become more responsible for shaping our own future." — Hillary Rodham Clinton

**910.** "I have always grown from my problems and challenges, from the things that don't work out, that's when I've really learned." — Carol Burnett

**911.** "If you want to see something done, just tell some human beings it can't be done. Make it known that it's impossible to fly to the moon, or run 100 meters in 9.9 seconds, or solve Fermat's Last Theorem. Remind the world that no one has ever hit 62 home runs in a season or stuffed 18 people into a Volkswagen. Dangle the undoable in front of the world. Then, consider it done." — Merrill Lynch advertisement

**912.** "Life's challenges are not supposed to paralyze you, they're supposed to help you discover who you are." — Bernice Johnson Reagon

913. "The marvelous richness of human experience would lose something of rewarding joy if there were no limitations to overcome. The hilltop hour would not be half so wonderful if there were no dark valleys to traverse." — Helen Keller

914. "Providence has hidden a charm in difficult undertakings, which is appreciated only by those who dare to grapple with them." — Anne-Sophie Swetchine

915. "There are no great people in this world, only great challenges which ordinary people rise to meet." — William Frederick Halsey, Jr.

916. "The ultimate measure of a man is not where he stands in moments of comfort and convenience, but where he stands in times of challenge and controversy."
— Martin Luther King, Jr.

photophilde/flickr
http://www.flickr.com/photos/82182478@N00/3533954656/in/pho tolist

917. "When we long for life without difficulties, remind us that oaks grow strong in contrary winds and diamonds are made under pressure." — Peter Marshall

918. "You must do the thing you think you cannot do." — Eleanor Roosevelt

919. "A candle loses nothing by lighting another candle." - Author Unknown

920. "A kindness done today is the surest way to a brighter tomorrow." - Author Unknown

921. "A knowledge of the path cannot be substituted for putting one foot in front of the other." - Author Unknown

922. "A person often meets his destiny on the road he took to avoid it." - Jean De La Fontaine

923. "A pessimist sees the difficulty in every opportunity, an optimist sees the opportunity in every difficulty." - Winston Churchill

924. "A ship in harbor is safe, but that is not what ships are built for." - William Shedd

925. "A stumble may prevent a fall." - English proverb

926. "Ability may get you to the top, but it takes character to keep you there." - John Wooden

927. "Aim at Heaven and you will get Earth thrown in. Aim at Earth and you get neither." - C.S.Lewis

928. "All of our dreams can come true -- if we have the courage to pursue them." - Walt Disney

929. "All riches have their origin in mind. Wealth is in ideas -- not money". - Robert Collier

930. "All the adversity I've had in my life, all my troubles and obstacles, have strengthened me. . . . You may not realize it when it happens, but a kick in the teeth may be the best thing in the world for you." - Walt Disney

931. "Always try to be a little kinder than is necessary." - James M. Barrie

932. "An effort made for the happiness of others lifts above ourselves." - Lydia Maria Child

933. "And what is as important as knowledge?" asked the mind. "Caring and seeing with the heart," answered the soul. - Author Unknown

934. "Any fact facing us is not as important as our attitude toward it, for that determines our success or failure." - Norman Vincent Peale

935. "Anyone who has accustomed himself to regard the life of any living creature as worthless is in danger of arriving also at the idea of worthless human lives." - Albert Schweitzer

936. "As long as you keep a person down, some part of you has to be down there to hold him down, so it means you cannot soar as you otherwise might." - Marian Anderson

937. "As long as you're actively pursuing your dream with a practical plan, you're still achieving, even if it feels as though you're

going nowhere fast. It's been my experience that at the very moment I feel like giving up, I'm only one step from a breakthrough. Hang on long enough and circumstances will change, too. Trust in yourself, your dream and Spirit." - Sarah Ban Breathnach

938. "Be inspired with the belief that life is a great and noble calling; not a mean and groveling thing that we are to shuffle through as we can, but an elevated and lofty destiny." - William E. Gladstone

939. "Be kind, for everyone you meet is fighting a hard battle." - Author Unknown

940. "Become a possibilitarian. No matter how dark things seem to be or actually are, raise your sights and see the possibilities -- always see them, for they're always there." - Norman Vincent Peale

941. "Begin doing what you want to do now. We are not living in eternity. We have only this moment, sparkling like a star in our hand -- and melting like a snowflake." - Marie Beyon Ray

942. "Begin somewhere. You cannot build a reputation on what you intend to do." - Liz Smith

943. "Careers, like rockets, don't always take off on schedule. The key is to keep working the engines." - Gary Sinise

944. "Character cannot be developed in ease and quiet. Only through experience of trial and suffering can the soul be strengthened, ambition inspired, and success achieved." - Helen Keller

945. "Cherish your visions and your dreams as they are the children of your soul; the blue-prints of your ultimate achievements." - Napoleon Hill

946. "Choose Life! Only that and always! At whatever risk, to let life leak out, to let it wear away by the mere passage of time, to withhold giving and spending it ... is to choose nothing." - Sister Helen Kelly

947. "Concentrate on where you want to go, not on what you fear." - Anthony Robbins

948. "Consult not your fears but your hopes and your dreams. Think not about your frustrations, but about your unfulfilled potential. Concern yourself not with what you tried and failed in, but with what it is still possible for you to do." - Pope John XXIII

949. "Courage is resistance to fear, mastery of fear -- not absence of fear. Except a creature be part coward it is not a compliment to say it is brave." - Mark Twain

950. "Courage is the power to let go of the familiar." - Raymond Lindquist

951. "Destiny is not a matter of chance; but a matter of choice. It is not a thing to be waited for. It is a thing to be achieved." - William Jennings Bryant

952. "Don't focus on the days when you failed. Focus on all of the days when you won. Keep a chart, monitor your successes, and don't give up! " - Robert Butterworth

953. "Don't judge each day by the harvest you reap, but by the seeds you plant." - Robert Louis Stevenson

954. "Don't let the fear of the time it will take to accomplish something stand in the way of your doing it. The time will pass anyway; we might just as well put that passing time to the best possible use." - Earl Nightingale

955. "Don't take life so seriously. It isn't permanent." - Author Unknown

956. "Dreams are renewable. No matter what our age or condition, there are still untapped possibilities within us and new beauty waiting to be born." - Dale Turner

957. "Duty makes us do things well, but love makes us do them beautifully." - Author Unknown

958. "Each moment is an opportunity to reveal a miracle. Grace is a wonderful quality of the Spirit. When it is manifested in our lives, it brings the energy that uplifts our vibrations and clears the inner barriers. To be in a state of gratefulness is to put into practice the certainty that if we knock the door will be opened, and if we ask it will be given unto us." - Sonia Café

959. "Either write something worth reading or do something worth writing." - Ben Franklin

960. "My life turned around when I began to believe in me." - Robert Schuller

961. "Every situation, properly perceived, becomes an opportunity." - Helen Schucman

962. "Failure is an event, never a person." - William D. Brown

963. "Failure is only the opportunity to begin again more intelligently." - Henry Ford

964. "Faith is to believe what you do not yet see; the reward for this faith is to see what you believe." - St. Augustine

965. "Fall seven times; stand up eight." - Japanese Proverb

966. "Forget past mistakes. Forget failures. Forget everything except what you're going to do now, and do it." - William Durant, founder of General Motors

967. "From what we get, we can make a living; what we give, however, makes a life." - Arthur Ashe

968. "Getting ahead in a difficult profession -- singing, acting, writing, whatever -- requires avid faith in yourself. You must be able to sustain yourself against staggering blows and unfair reversals. When I think back to those first couple of years in Rome, those endless rejections, without a glimmer of encouragement from anyone, all those failed screen tests, and yet I never let my desire slide away from me, my belief in myself, and what I felt I could achieve." - Sophia Loren

969. "Go confidently in the direction of your dreams. Live the life you've imagined." - Henry David Thoreau

970. "Goals determine what you are going to be." - Julius Irving

971. "God loves us the way we are, but He loves us too much to leave us that way." - Leighton Ford

972. "Gratitude unlocks the fullness of life. It turns what we have into enough, and more. It turns denial into acceptance, chaos to order, confusion to clarity. It can turn a meal into a feast, a house into a home, a stranger into a friend. Gratitude makes sense of our past, brings peace for today, and creates a vision for tomorrow." - Melody Beattie

973. "Great works are performed not by strength but by perseverance." - Samuel Johnson

974. "Have a heart that never hardens, a temper that never tires, and a touch that never hurts." - Charles Dickens

975. "Have faith in your dreams and someday, your rainbow will come shining through. No matter how your heart is grieving, if you keep believing, the dream that you wish will come true." – Cinderella

976. "He is well paid that is well satisfied." - William Shakespeare

977. "He who endures conquers." - Italian Proverb

978. "He who loses money, loses much; he who loses a friend, loses much more; he who loses faith, loses all." - Author Unknown

979. "Here is a test to find out whether your mission in life is complete. If you're alive, it isn't." - Richard Bach, Illusions

980. "Hope is the companion of power, and mother of success; for who so hopes strongly has within him the gift of miracles." - Samuel Smiles

981. "I am thankful for this most amazing day; for the leaping greenly spirits of trees, and a blue true dream of sky, and for everything which is natural, which is infinite, which is yes." - E.E. Cummings

982. "I believe in the sun even when it's not shining. I believe in love even when not feeling it. I believe in God even when He is silent." – Unknown

983. "I think the purpose of life is to be useful, to be responsible, to be honorable, to be compassionate. It is, above all, to matter, to

count, to stand for something, to have made some difference that you lived at all." - Leo C. Rosten

**984.** "I don't know the key to success, but the key to failure is trying to please everybody." - Bill Cosby

**985.** "I exist as I am - That is enough." - Walt Whitman

**986.** "I was taught that the way of progress is neither swift nor easy." - Marie Curie

**987.** "I will persist until I succeed. Always will I take another step. If that is of no avail I will take another, and yet another. In truth, one step at a time is not too difficult. . . . I know that small attempts, repeated, will complete any undertaking." - Og Mandino

**988.** "If I have the belief that I can do it, I shall surely acquire the capacity to do it even if I may not have it at the beginning." - Mahatma Gandhi

**989.** "I will be bigger than you. You cannot defeat me." - Ann Landers

**990.** "If people knew how hard I worked at my art, they would not consider me a genius." – Michelangelo

**991.** "If someone betrays you once, it is his fault; if he betrays you twice, it is your fault." - Author Unknown

**992.** "If we all did the things we are capable of, we would astound ourselves." - Thomas Edison

**993.** "If you believe in your heart that you are right, you must fight with all your might to do it your way. Only dead fish swim with the stream all the time." - Linda Ellerbee

994. "If you think you can, you can. And if you think you can't, you're right." - Mary Kay Ash

995. "If you want a quality, act as if you already had it. Try the "as if" technique." - William James

996. "In the world there is nothing more submissive and weak than water. Yet for attacking that which is hard and strong nothing can surpass it." - Lao Tzu

997. "It is funny about life: if you refuse to accept anything but the very best you will very often get it." - W. Somerset Maugham

998. "It is not because things are difficult that we do not dare, it is because we do not dare that they are difficult." - Seneca

999. "The roots of true achievement lie in the will to become the best that you can become." - Harold Taylor

1000. "Keep away from people who try to belittle your ambitions. Small people always do that, but the really great make you feel that you, too, can become great." - Mark Twain

CPSIA information can be obtained at www.ICGtesting.com
Printed in the USA
LVOW10s2220120216

474886LV00026B/763/P